EMIL BRUNNER

Makers of the Modern Theological Mind

Bob E. Patterson, Editor

KARL BARTH by *David L. Mueller*
DIETRICH BONHOEFFER by *Dallas M. Roark*
RUDOLF BULTMANN by *Morris Ashcraft*
CHARLES HARTSHORNE by *Alan Gragg*
WOLFHART PANNENBERG by *Don Olive*
TEILHARD DE CHARDIN by *Doran McCarty*
EMIL BRUNNER by *J. Edward Humphrey*
MARTIN BUBER by *Stephen M. Panko*
SÖREN KIERKEGAARD by *Elmer Duncan*
REINHOLD NIEBUHR by *Bob E. Patterson*

Makers of the Modern Theological Mind

Bob E. Patterson, Editor

EMIL BRUNNER

by J. Edward Humphrey

Word Books, Publisher, Waco, Texas

First Printing—March 1976
Second Printing—December 1976
Third Printing—March 1977

EMIL BRUNNER

Library of Congress catalog card number: 75-36186
ISBN #0-87680-453-9
Printed in the United States of America.

Unless otherwise noted, all Scripture quotations are taken from the American Standard Version, 1901.

The quotation marked RSV is from The Revised Standard Version of the Bible, copyrighted 1946, 1952, and © 1971, 1973 by the Division of Christian Education of the National Council of the Churches of Christ in the U.S.A. and is used by permission.

Grateful acknowledgment is hereby made for permission to quote from the following published works:

To The Macmillan Company, New York, for permission to quote from *The Theology of Emil Brunner*, edited by Charles W. Kegley, copyright 1962 by Charles W. Kegley.

To The Westminster Press, Philadelphia, for permission to quote from *The Christian Doctrine of God*, by Emil Brunner, translated by Olive Wyon, copyright 1950 by W. L. Jenkins; *The Christian Doctrine of Creation and Redemption*, by Emil Brunner, translated by Olive Wyon, first published in English, 1952, by Lutterworth Press, London; *The Christian Doctrine of the Church, Faith, and the Consummation*, by Emil Brunner, translated by David Cairns in collaboration with T. H. L. Parker, copyright 1962 by Lutterworth Press; *Man in Revolt*, by Emil Brunner, translated by Olive Wyon, copyright 1947 by W. L. Jenkins; *The Divine Imperative*, by Emil Brunner, translated by Olive Wyon, copyright 1947 by W. L. Jenkins; *Revelation and Reason*, by Emil Brunner, translated by Olive Wyon, copyright 1946 by W. L. Jenkins; *The Mediator*, by Emil Brunner, translated by Olive Wyon, copyright 1947, by W. L. Jenkins; *Truth as Encounter*, by Emil Brunner (revised and enlarged edition of *The Divine-Human Encounter)*, translated by Amandus W. Loos, and David Cairns in consultation with T. H. L. Parker, copyright 1943 by The Westminster Press, and 1964 by W. L. Jenkins; *The Misunderstanding of the Church*, by Emil Brunner, translated by Harold Knight, copyright 1953 by W. L. Jenkins; *Eternal Hope*, by Emil Brunner, translated by Harold Knight, published, 1954, by The Westminster Press.

For Rachel
dear companion in
life and faith

Contents

Editor's Preface

Who are the thinkers that have shaped Christian theology in our time? This series tries to answer that question by providing a reliable guide to the ideas of the men who have significantly charted the theological seas of our century. In the current revival of theology, these books will give a new generation the opportunity to be exposed to significant minds. They are not meant, however, to be a substitute for a careful study of the original works of these makers of the modern theological mind.

This series is not for the lazy. Each major theologian is examined carefully and critically—his life, his theological method, his most germinal ideas, his weaknesses as a thinker, his place in the theological spectrum, and his chief contribution to the climate of theology today. The books are written with the assumption that laymen will read them and enter into the theological dialogue that is so necessary to the church as a whole. At the same time they are carefully enough designed to give assurance to a Ph.D. student in theology preparing for his preliminary exams.

Each author in the series is a professional scholar and theologian in his own right. All are specialists on, and in some cases have studied with, the theologians about whom they write. Welcome to the series.

BOB E. PATTERSON, Editor
Baylor University

Preface

The invitation to undertake an analysis of the theology of Emil Brunner evokes a glad response on my part. It affords an opportunity to reflect more deeply upon the thought of one who has been a truly formative influence in my own theological development. During my student days in the nineteen forties, I listened with uncommon intensity to a series of lectures by this great man and realized that I was being exposed to an unusual mind and spirit. In the succeeding months and years, the reading of one and another of his many books always left me with a growing sense of affinity for his way of thinking, the result being that his *Dogmatics* eventually provided, in large measure, the basic structure of introductory courses in my own teaching of theology.

On the other hand, this project cannot but leave me with some apprehension from the very beginning. There is the twofold obligation to be objectively critical in analysis and at the same time try to do justice to the thought and intention of a Christian thinker of Brunner's stature. Distinguished theologians have reacted in one way and another to various aspects of Brunner's thought. This little volume will have served its supreme purpose if it assists in attracting others to a first-hand reading of Brunner's own works and thereby to a deeper desire for that exposure to truth which he describes as "encounter."

My appreciation is hereby acknowledged for all who have

promoted or shown an interest in this work from its inception. These include Dr. Bob E. Patterson of Baylor University, general editor of this series, who invited me to undertake it, Dr. Richard B. Cunningham, my colleague at Golden Gate Baptist Theological Seminary, who first suggested that I prepare the volume on Brunner, and Ms. Mary Ruth Howes, senior editor at Word Books, Publisher, who has made numerous suggestions for improving the final form of this work. Special thanks are hereby extended to the several ladies in the secretarial pool at Golden Gate Baptist Theological Seminary who have patiently and efficiently converted the handwritten manuscript to typed form. And finally, my deepest gratitude is reserved for my wife, Rachel, who inspires and encourages me in every human endeavor.

I. Emil Brunner

HIS FORMATION AS A THEOLOGIAN

The Biographical Context

An extended biography of Emil Brunner has never been published. Fortunately, he left two brief autobiographical sketches which portray the more significant aspects of his development, together with the contributing factors as he saw them. The first, entitled "A Spiritual Autobiography," appeared in the *Japan Christian Quarterly* in 1955.[1] The second, entitled "Intellectual Autobiography,"[2] was a considerably enlarged and extended revision of the first sketch and appeared seven years later at the beginning of a symposium on Brunner's theology in the series The Library of Living Theology (vol. III). Other significant bits of information have been supplied by incidental statements in his other writings and in those of his former students and others.

Emil Brunner was born December 23, 1889, at Winterthur, near Zurich, Switzerland. His early education was completed at the *Gymnasium* in Zurich in 1908. Thereafter, he studied at the Universities of Zurich and Berlin, receiving his Doctor of Theology degree from the former in 1913. At the height of his career, several distinguished universities on the Continent, in Britain, and in America honored him, and themselves, in conferring honorary degrees upon him. In 1913–14, he spent some time in England teaching languages in a high school at Leeds and becoming more proficient in the use of English. Upon the outbreak of the First World War in 1914, Brunner returned to his native land, where he served for a time in the Swiss militia.

Brunner's pastoral experience began with six months of service as vicar in Hermann Kutter's *Neumünster* congregation at Zurich. In 1916, he was called as pastor of a small congregation in the mountain village of Obstalden in the Canton of Glarus. While there, he married Margrit Lauterburg, a niece of Hermann Kutter, in 1917. His pastoral ministry at Obstalden was interrupted in 1919 for a year of study at Union Theological Seminary in New York City and was resumed in 1920. From 1924 to 1955, he occupied the Chair of Systematic and Practical Theology at the University of Zurich. During these three decades, he made frequent lecture-tours to centers of learning on the Continent of Europe, in Britain, and in America. And in 1938–39, he was visiting professor at Princeton Theological Seminary. The climax of his career, as he saw it, came near the end of his life when he spent two years (1953–55) helping to build up the new International Christian University in Tokyo.

On his return journey from Japan to Zurich in 1955, Brunner suffered a cerebral hemorrhage, with permanent impairment of speech and limb. In spite of a series of subsequent strokes, he enjoyed a measure of health for several more years. On the morning of April 6, 1966, following a last severe illness of more than three months during which "he found much strength and comfort in Romans Eight," he made the final "encounter" with his Lord.[3]

The Intellectual and Spiritual Development[4]

Brunner understood his intellectual and spiritual development in part as a deposit of certain streams of truth which flowed into his life, one might say, as an accident of birth. The first of these was related to his Swiss nationality. On his father's side, the lineage reached back through "an unbroken line of Zurich farmers" to the time of the Reformation. All his life he believed that the ideals of democracy instilled in him from this "oldest republic of our world" were germane to his thought.

A second stream of spiritual truth which helped to mold his thought was the Reformed tradition, extending back to Ulrich Zwingli (1484–1531). Brunner's maternal grandfather was a Reformed minister, and his own parents were devout representatives of that tradition, though his father had descended from a family of nonbelievers. He was himself a member of that branch of the Christian church from early childhood to the end of his life.

The religious Socialist Movement also provided a powerful formative influence on Brunner's thought. This movement reached Switzerland from Germany, in a revised form, through the instrumentality of two south German Lutheran pastors, Johann Christoph Blumhardt (1805–1880) and his son Christoph Blumhardt (1842–1919). In Germany, religious socialism in the latter part of the nineteenth century passed through a variety of phases. In a few of the churches, pastors with strong ethical passion gave a social interpretation to Christianity and pressed for political reforms in behalf of the industrial masses. They were stoutly opposed by the conservative wing of Lutheranism, which insisted upon the separation of political and spiritual spheres. Eventually, an academic form of religious socialism was being advocated in the context of the liberal theology of such men as Adolf von Harnack at the University of Berlin and Wilhelm Hermann at the University of Marburg. All the while, the Blumhardts were striving to give the movement a firm Christological foundation and to place it in the context of a dynamic life in the Spirit.[5]

Brunner knew the younger Blumhardt personally, but Blumhardt's influence on him was mainly indirect, coming through two of Blumhardt's Swiss followers. One of these was Hermann Kutter (1863–1931), pastor of the *Neumünster* congregation in Zurich, under whom Brunner was catechized and whom he regarded as "the greatest man" he ever knew. The other was

Leonhard Ragaz (1868–1945), one of Brunner's teachers at the University of Zurich. Through the influence of these men, Brunner came to the conclusion that "the so-called dialectical theology," with which he was to be engaged for the remainder of his life, had its origin, not in any theological or philosophical system of thought, but in the reality of the Holy Spirit.

There were also certain events and spheres of influence which converged to help mold his life and thought. Some of these belonged to the earlier stages of his development, while others provided the stimulus for new vitality and insights in the latter half of his life. Prominent among these was the formation of a small circle of theologians with whom Brunner became loosely associated in the early 1920s, who more or less centered around Karl Barth.

Among the men of this group, there were already indications of individuality of potentially wide divergence. This circle of thinkers included Karl Barth, Eduard Thurneysen, Friedrich Gogarten, Georg Merz, and Rudolf Bultmann. The chief literary organ for the dissemination of their views was a religious journal entitled *Zwischen den Zeiten* (Between the Times). Disillusionment brought on by the catastrophe of the First World War had left these men with the shared conviction that the very foundation and aims of the reigning religious socialism with its presuppositions must be reexamined. As a result, a theological revolution took place largely through the columns of that journal. Brunner was one of the more outspoken contenders that this examination must begin with the message of Christ itself. The line of thought developed by this group has been variously designated as the theology of crisis, dialectical theology, neo-orthodoxy, and Barthian theology. In Brunner's opinion, each of these names "is both significant and misleading." In his own context, he made free use of the first two and took strong exceptions to the last.

The basic direction of Brunner's theology had already been determined before he encountered Karl Barth; and therefore when Barth's *Römerbrief (Epistle to the Romans)* was written in 1918, Brunner hailed it as "a forceful confirmation" of his own thought. He believed that in his own published review of this book, he was the first to call attention to "its epoch-making character." As he pointed out, both Barth and Thurneysen also came from that circle of influence emanating from Blumhardt and Kutter. He contended however that from the beginning he had taken a position independent of that of Barth and that this independence in later years became more pronounced.

Without being aware of an earlier revival of the study of Luther in Sweden, Brunner, Barth and Thurneysen all began a study of this sixteenth-century Reformer, with what Brunner described as "incredible joy and enthusiasm." They later focused in a similar way upon the works of Calvin, "with less joy but equal reverence." They all believed that essential insights into the biblical message had been briefly recovered by the Reformers, but that many of these had become blurred if not actually lost in the intervening time. So great was Brunner's conviction of this that one cannot read far in his *Dogmatics* without being aware of the presence of basic Reformation thought just beneath the surface in much of his theology. Any authority which he attributed to the Reformers, however, was contingent upon their faithfulness to the biblical revelation.

Of particular importance to Brunner in the 1930s were two "spiritual factors" which, in spite of their apparent diversity, he believed to be somehow closely related in their contribution to his thought. The first of these was the Oxford Group Movement, which reached Switzerland in 1931. Seeing its potential for the revitalization of both the church and theology, Brunner was soon drawn into the movement. And while he was aware of certain excesses and possible dangers, he became an enthusiastic participant and supporter of the movement. Its engagement of the spiritual activity of the entire Christian community, especially the laymen, seemed to him to recover a dimension of the New Testament church which had been lost for most of Christian history. He felt that for the first time he was now aware of "the close connection between spiritual reality and fellowship or communion."

The second spiritual factor of this period was the "I-Thou" philosophy of Ferdinand Ebner (1882–1931) and Martin Buber (1878–1965), which they in turn owed to insights received from Sören Kierkegaard and the Bible. This philosophy helped Brunner to work out his anthropology on a plane above the traditional rationalistic thought-scheme of object and subject, and enabled him to understand more clearly the biblical concept of man as responsible being before God. The human person was here understood in his primary relation to the divine Thou; and at the same time a clear distinction was drawn between this I-Thou relation and the I-It relation to things.

From this understanding of man Brunner was led to consider what he regarded as a fundamental question, namely, the biblical concept of truth. He dealt with this problem in a series of lectures in 1938, concluding that one could not understand the gospel apart from being personally engaged in an I-Thou encounter with God. He expressed this new insight in the phrase, "truth as encounter," which was not only adopted as the title for these lectures in published form, but was to appear again and again in his later *Dogmatics*. He referred to it as the "lodestar" of his "theological thinking" from 1938 onward.

The Literary Production

Near the close of his life, and by request, Brunner gave a brief resumé of his intellectual development. Here, he made unmistakably clear his sense of priorities. From the beginning, his labors in the areas of theology and philosophy were "strictly subordinated to the proclamation of the Gospel," for he regarded himself above all else "a preacher of the Good News." Theologizing and philosophizing were of value only insofar as they in fact aided in the understanding and communication of the divine Word. He professed to regard all his books as "a paraphrase of Romans 1:16." [6]

Nevertheless, every year without exception for at least forty-nine years, Brunner went to press with his contributions to serious theology. We are fortunate in having a bibliography of his writings from 1914 to 1962 prepared by his wife. Her list, comprising both books and journal articles, numbers 396 items —and he was not yet finished. During this period, at least twenty-three of his books were made available in English,[7] and a few others were yet to be translated. Limitations of space in this volume necessitate limiting the descriptions that follow to only the more central of these works.

Brunner's first publication was his doctoral dissertation in 1914, *Das Symbolische in der Religiösen Erkenntnis* (The Symbolic Element in Religious Knowledge).[8] This work represents a search for what he called "a scientifically satisfying formulation" of his faith. It was written at a time when he was reacting to the ideological framework of the Religious Socialist Movement and was deeply engrossed in philosophical studies, especially the epistemological works of Immanuel Kant and the phenomenological works of Edmund Husserl. At the same time, a study of social economy had awakened in him a concern for social ethics. But above all of these interests was a fundamental absorption in the question of God.[9]

In 1921, he wrote a work entitled *Erlebnis, Erkenntnis und Glaube* (Experience, Knowledge and Faith) [10] which he later referred to as his "inauguratory thesis." [11] This work was a radical criticism of those abstract systems which had endeavored to combine experience and knowledge apart from faith and which had pressed the philosophy of identity to the point that a mediator was no longer needed.[12] A more extensive work, *Die Mystik und das Wort* (Mysticism and the Word) appeared in 1924.[13] This book was a critical assessment of the theology of Friedrich Schleiermacher. As such, it was the first of a series of works by Brunner which were at once an attack upon liberal theology and an attempt to present the gospel to a generation which regarded itself as too intelligent to believe the New Testament message.[14] The publication of these two books led to

Brunner's appointment to the Chair of Systematic and Practical Theology at the University of Zurich.

Most of Brunner's previous works had been composed in what he referred to as "the solitude of my mountain parsonage"[15] and were sharply critical of modern theology. But now he faced the exacting responsibilities of a university teacher of theology and found it necessary to reassess the approach he would take to the task before him. Meanwhile, Karl Barth reviewed Brunner's analysis of Schleiermacher's theology and helped him to see the necessity of combining with his criticism a positive and constructive contribution "along the right path."[16] This new perspective was soon to become apparent in his writings.

In 1927, he published two works which reflect his enlarged understanding of the theological task both by the nature and scope of their substance and by the order of publication. The first was his *Religionsphilosophie evangelischer Theologie (The Philosophy of Religion from the Standpoint of Protestant Theology)*.[17] This work was intended as a systematic exposition of the underlying philosophy of the "theology of crisis," a sort of "prolegomena" to that larger task. As such, it was proper that it be published first. But prolegomena must be accompanied by "at least some specimen of actual theological work" in order to be rightly understood.[18] Therefore, it was quickly followed by *Der Mittler (The Mediator)*.[19] *The Mediator* was the first attempt by anyone to treat the doctrine of Christ "in terms of the dialectical theology."[20] With this monograph the Christological center of Brunner's theology was clearly established.

With the publication of *The Mediator*, Brunner was immediately in wide demand as a visiting lecturer. In the autumn of the year 1928, he visited seven different theological schools in the United States, presenting in whole or in part the essays which comprise his volume entitled *The Theology of Crisis*.[21] These lectures were a popular presentation of a broad spectrum of his thought and served to introduce the dialectical theology to the American scene. They were followed in the autumn of

1929 by another lecture-tour to various universities in Holland. The lectures presented in these schools, combined with others, compose his work entitled *Gott und Mensch (God and Man).*[22] The significance of these lectures lies in the evidence they present that Brunner was already wrestling with "the problem of the nature of personal being,"[23] a theme which was to be at the heart of his writings for the remainder of his life.

A further lecture-tour in 1931 took him to London, Glasgow, and Edinburgh where he presented a series of essays which were published under the title, *The Word and the World.*[24] The aim of these lectures was twofold. The primary purpose was to help remove the barriers encountered by modern scientifically oriented minds when confronted by the biblical message, clothed as it is in the external garb of a primitive world-view. A secondary purpose was to further clarify the nature and aims of the dialectical theology.[25] Similar lecture-tours were to follow in Hungary, Denmark, Finland, and Sweden.[26]

Toward the close of the twenties, Brunner's attention was drawn to what seemed to him a foreboding phenomenon in the political realm, namely, the emergence of the totalitarian state. It was already present in the guise of communism and was soon to appear in the forms of fascism and national socialism, all of which he quickly recognized as being far more than mere political or economic entities. He saw each of these as "an intellectual-spiritual power, based on atheistic principles" and embodying far-reaching implications for the concept of man as person before God. He began to ponder this problem in the preparation of lectures on Christian ethics, with a growing conviction that the new phenomenon was antithetical to the view of man as presented in the New Testament idea of the church.[27] Preoccupation with these matters involved him in the various facets of a Christian anthropology which were to absorb his major energies for a full decade.

Ethical concern had been apparent from the beginning in all of his writings; but his one major contribution in this area appeared in 1932 under the title *Das Gebot und die Ordnungen*

(The Divine Imperative).[28] *The Divine Imperative* has been one of Brunner's most widely discussed books. He developed his view of Christian ethics around two governing ideas. The first was the primary command of God to love. All other commands were understood as derivative from this supreme command. The second idea was expressed in the phrase *orders of creation,* by which he designated five dimensions of community which are fundamental to human existence. In each of these spheres we are confronted by God's will. The major part of this work deals with the meaning of community according to God's purpose of love in these spheres.

Concentration upon the problems of anthropology quickly led to a consideration of the question of the inherent capacities of man, especially with regard to grace and revelation. As early as 1929, divergence of opinion at this point, and with it a growing mutual apprehension, seems to have arisen between Brunner and Barth. Brunner began to speak of a "point of contact" for the gospel in the consciousness of the natural man. He went on to speak of what he called "the other task of theology,"[29] which was to properly relate special revelation to this element in the human consciousness. Barth took strong exception to this view, and a series of literary exchanges took place. All attempts at clarification failed, resulting in an open controversy which was to become one of the most famous theological disputes of this century. The rift between the two men came to a climax in 1934 when Brunner published a small work entitled *Natur und Gnade. Zum Gespräch mit Karl Barth* (Nature and Grace. Discussion with Karl Barth)[30] and Barth replied with a blistering article under the forceful caption, *Nein!* (No!).[31] The breach effected by this last exchange was not healed until near the end of their lives.

Under the impulse of his experience with the Oxford Group Movement, Brunner published two small works in 1935 which were consciously related to the church in action. One of them, *Vom Werk des Heiligen Geistes* (On the Work of the Holy Spirit),[32] is a treatment of the work of God in three dimensions of human existence: with reference to the past it is a work of faith; with reference to the present it is a work of love; with reference to the future it is a work of hope. This book was apparently never published in English. The other book was "a small popular compendium of theology" entitled *Unser Glaube (Our Faith)*.[33] Referring to this book near the end of his life, Brunner recalled that it had been translated into nineteen different languages, and he spoke of it as "one of the dearest fruits of my life-work."[34]

During this period, Brunner labored under the growing conviction that every political and social system is determined by some underlying view of man. Reflecting on this fact and drawing upon the insights gained from the social thought of Max Weber and the I-Thou philosophy of Sören Kierkegaard, Ferdinand Ebner, and Martin Buber, he undertook to work out a Christian doctrine of man. This work was published in 1937 under the title, *Der Mensch im Widerspruch (Man in Revolt)*.[35] As with *The Mediator*, this also was a first attempt to deal with a major doctrine on the basis of the post-World War I reorientation of theology.[36] He regarded the problem of anthropology as among the most important in theology, holding that only in the realization of self-knowledge does faith come into being. At the heart of his argument was the view of man as responsible being before God, but as a matter of actual fact, man in revolt against his Creator. The implications of this predicament for communion on the divine and human levels were here explored in man's various relations. Brunner is said to have spoken of this book as his chief contribution to theology.[37]

These anthropological studies culminated in the "even more fundamental question" of truth. In the fall of 1937, Brunner delivered a series of lectures at the University of Uppsala, Sweden, bearing the title, *Wahrheit als Begegnung (Truth as Encounter)*.[38] In preparation for these lectures, he began with a suggestion made to him when the invitation to present them was given. Professor A. Runestam of Uppsala suggested that he take as his theme the subject, "Objectivism and Subjectivism in Theology and the Church." As he reflected on this theme, Brunner became convinced that our understanding of the gospel and of the task of the church is still "burdened with the subject-object antithesis," which was originally an accretion from Greek philosophy. Such a view entails the idea of truth by abstraction. He concluded that by contrast, the biblical understanding of truth is "truth as encounter." This seemed to be a clarification of the insight toward which he had been groping for years. From that time onward, his entire labors in dogmatics were guided by the vision of the God who communicates himself. He was now more convinced than ever that revelation rather than reason is the indispensable starting point in all valid theological endeavor. With this positive insight, he was now ready to turn his energies to the process of a distillation of his previous theological soundings, looking toward the presentation of a comprehensive Dogmatics.

In 1941, Brunner published his *Offenbarung und Vernunft: Die Lehre von der christlichen Glaubenserkenntnis (Revelation and Reason: The Christian Doctrine of Faith and Knowledge)*,[39] which was designed to serve as prolegomena to his proposed Dogmatics. The essential fact with which that book was concerned was the insight that a knowledge of God can be had only through and insofar as there is a divine self-disclosure. In the ensuing years, he was preoccupied with many endeavors, including the writing of other books, so that his *Dogmatics*, in three volumes, did not reach completion until 1960. In 1946, the first volume of the *Dogmatics* appeared under the title, *Die christliche Lehre von Gott (The Christian Doctrine of God)*.[40] The second volume was published in 1950, bearing the title, *Die christliche Lehre von Schöpfung und Erlösung (The Christian Doctrine of Creation and Redemption)*.[41] The third volume, which was produced after he had lost the use of his writing hand because of a cerebral hemorrhage, finally appeared in 1960—*Die christliche Lehre von der Kirche, vom Glauben, und von der Vollendung (The Christian Doctrine of the Church, Faith and Consummation)*.[42]

When he began the publication of his *Dogmatics*, Brunner had been giving university lectures in the subject for more than twenty years. He had already put forth several widely acclaimed monographs on key doctrines. During this time, he had attempted "to recast the doctrinal material as a whole" nearly a dozen times.[43] When his scheme was at last sufficiently refined for his purpose, he saw it as a vehicle for summing up his previous work in the area of biblical theology. In the attempt to get back to biblical principles and to restore to its central place "the question of the nature of faith," he now set his entire theology within the magnificent framework of "the divine self-communication."[44]

This schematic view of divine self-communication was drawn up in four parts. Beginning with its eternal foundation, he discussed in the first part the nature and will of God. The second part discussed its historical realization through creation and redemption. The third part treated God's "self-representation through the Holy Spirit," that is, the church and the new life in Christ. In the fourth part he discussed the "consummation in eternity of the divine self-communication," a treatment of matters related to the Kingdom of God and eschatology.

In the midst of his labors on the *Dogmatics*, Brunner found time to produce several other significant volumes. The first of these was *Das Wort Gottes und der moderne Mensch (The Word of God and Modern Man)*.[45] Here Brunner undertakes to engage modern man (especially unbelieving man) in conversation as to who he is in the light of his being in the Word of God. During this time, Brunner also delivered the Gifford Lectures at The University of St. Andrews on the subject *Christianity and Civilization*, which were published in two volumes in consecutive years.[46]

Brunner's participation in ecumenical discussions led him to prepare two other volumes in the early 1950s. The first of these was his contribution to the question being asked on every hand, "What Is the Church?" *Das Missverständnis der Kirche (The Misunderstanding of the Church)*[47] expressed the conviction that both in theology and in all forms of institutional structure, the unique character of the *ęcclēsia* (church) of the New Testament had been seriously distorted through a loss of the spirit of Christ.

His other ecumenical contribution of this period came in connection with the theological preparation for the second gathering of the World Council of Churches in 1954. The theme of that Council meeting was "Christ the Hope of the World." Brunner's work in this connection bore the title, *Das Ewige als Zukunft und Gegenwart* (The Eternal as Future and Present, published in English as *Eternal Hope*).[48] Brunner sought in this work to treat the main lines of the eschatology of the New Testament free from what he regarded as "the inadequate temporal conceptions of traditional theology." [49]

His final literary effort returned to the theme which he regarded as basic to all his theological work, namely, the biblical in contrast to all other conceptions of truth. This was a second edition of his earlier work which in translation had borne the inadequate title *The Divine-Human Encounter*. The title for this final edition in English went back to the equivalent of the German title of the first edition, namely, *Truth as Encounter*. The main body of this material was unaltered, but Brunner added a lengthy introductory section (fifty-five pages) in which he attempted to situate that earlier work "within the context of the general philosophical problem of truth," [50] and set forth "the Christian concept of truth in its antithesis to the naturalistic-positivistic and idealistic-speculative concepts." [51] By omitting this material in the earlier edition, he felt that he had made an emphasis which was a necessary corrective to the traditional understanding of truth. Now that the point had been made, he felt that this further word was in order to give balance and perspective to his comprehensive labor of the years.

HIS PLACE IN MODERN THEOLOGY

Among the great system-builders of Christian theology in this century, Emil Brunner holds a place of unquestioned eminence.

His name was associated from the beginning with the half-dozen or so thinkers who dramatically recharted the course of Christian thought in this century. After the meteoric appearance of Karl Barth on the theological horizon in 1918, a whole generation became accustomed to hearing the names "Barth and Brunner" listed as a pair—and a pair with whom to reckon.[52] Their role in exposing the inadequacy of the liberal theology in which they had been trained was without parallel, even among the distinguished circle of thinkers with whom their names are commonly associated.

Brunner remained at the forefront of theological scholarship for more than thirty-five years, relentlessly interpreting the Christian faith to the mind of modern man, both Occidental and Oriental. Perhaps no other theologian of this century has demonstrated a comparable ability to address the generality of modern men so directly and comprehensively. Almost an entire generation of theological students received their basic training in some kind of reaction to his system as a whole or to various aspects of it. As is often pointed out, the very titles of his books have become familiar modes of expression of key ideas in twentieth-century theology.

Always the exponent of a living faith, Brunner occupied a position which was sensitive to the entire spectrum of theological ferment, without losing his passionate concern for what may be called the perennial theology. He was no innovator, nor did he aspire to be. In relation to his contemporaries, Brunner has always represented what has been referred to as a balanced or middle way. He has shown an unusual sensitivity to vibrant issues, past, present, and future. His influence was disseminated not only through numerous lucidly written books and journal articles, but also by distinguished performance in classroom and pulpit, on lecture platform, and at conference table in many parts of the world.

Few theologians have achieved the superb style of Emil Brunner. His platform lectures, his dogmatic compositions, and his published sermons are widely acclaimed for the clarity, the conciseness, and the simplicity with which he handled the profundities of the faith. He was a model of communication, as is attested by the unusual holding power of his books. Several of his monographs were held in almost unrivaled esteem for three decades and more. The more central of his works had the good fortune of being translated into English at a relatively early date following original publication.

It was Brunner who first introduced the "new theology" to the English-speaking world. And during the ensuing years, he spent far more time in England and America than did any other European representative of the distinguished original circle of neo-orthodox theologians. Even those students who converged on Switzerland from various parts of the world expressly to study under his famous compatriot at Basel usually found their way to Brunner's classroom in Zurich as well.

Finally, Brunner has been characterized as "an ecumenical theologian *par excellence*." [53] Beginning in 1930 and continuing for the remainder of his life, he worked assiduously with various work groups within the ecumenical movement, serving on both the Life and Work and the Faith and Order Commissions. In this capacity, he participated in the theological discussions on the church in 1937 at the World Church Conference in Oxford which marked the final preparation for the formation of the World Council of Churches in 1948.

II. The Foundation of Christian Faith and Knowledge

THE NEED FOR PROLEGOMENA

Among the major developments in the theological task of modern times is the attention given to prolegomena—that is, to preliminary considerations which have a bearing on the understanding and the performance of theology. One might even contend with some validity that this is a distinctive feature of modern theology. The necessity for this formal addition, however, was already inherent in the basic reorientation of thought inaugurated by the Renaissance, affecting both phenomenological [1] and epistemological [2] concerns.

From the time of Constantine onward, the presuppositions and boundaries of theological reflection had been fairly sharply defined and controlled. With the Renaissance, the ground was laid for the effective undermining of authoritative institutional control of theology. The immediate results were apparent mainly in the form of open questions as to the nature and purpose of theology and as to the presuppositions underlying theological knowledge. But with the impact of modern science and philosophy, the need for prolegomena became compelling during the seventeenth century and has continued as a necessary feature of the theological task ever since. In the modern world it has become increasingly apparent that there are fundamental questions which must be dealt with before one plunges into a discussion of particular doctrinal concerns. Among these are questions having to do with such matters as the theologian's claims to truth, the relation between revelation and reason, and the problem of natural theology.

THE QUESTION OF TRUTH

Throughout his long literary career, Brunner manifested absorbing and sustained interest in the problem of truth. For him, the possibility of a knowledge of truth lay in the juxtaposition of revelation and reason—an arrangement very positively fixed in that order. Quite varied but systematic treatment of this subject is especially pronounced in three of his works which appeared when he was at the peak of his theological production: *Truth as Encounter, Revelation and Reason,* and *The Christian Doctrine of God.*

Brunner's understanding of truth was brought into sharp focus again near the end of his life in an exchange of ideas with Paul Tillich. In a symposium on Brunner's theology, Tillich contributed a chapter under the title, "Some Questions on Brunner's Epistemology." Here, Tillich asserted that Brunner had developed a theological theory of knowledge, which he went on to describe as biblical, existentialist, and "adequate to the subject matter with which theology has to deal." Tillich believed, however, that this epistemology was deficient in certain respects, particularly with regard to semantics, the use of symbolic language, the concern of natural theology, and the proper view of non-Christian religions.[3] In reply, Brunner stated categorically that he had not developed any epistemology, considering that a problem for Christian philosophy and not one for theology. With that assertion, he moved on to point out the fundamental difference between his understanding of truth and that which is based on objective knowledge. In no case, he said, may the theologian "incorporate faith into or subordinate it to a philosophical epistemology." [4]

THE PROBLEM OF REVELATION AND REASON

With that critical exchange of outlook, we are already at the heart of Brunner's understanding of revelation and reason in the development of Christian theology. He speaks of the proper relation between revelation and reason as "the fundamental problem" of all theology. In his own work, he begins with an effort to situate his thought firmly and decisively upon the historical fact of the self-revelation of God; and he never really departs from that theme. For him, the divine revelation "is the truth." It alone is "the ground and the norm, as well as the content" of the church's message.[5] The duty of the Christian theologian, therefore, is to reflect upon the revelation of God in Christ until all of his doctrinal formulation is a faithful expression of it. In his own case, when he had set forth his understanding of revelation, the main lines were already drawn for the entire corpus of his *Dogmatics.*

Revelation in Biblical Thought

For Brunner, the concept of revelation in some form or other is fundamental to religion in general and is as widespread as the belief in God. In a unique way, it belongs also to the biblical faith. There is in fact no single word in either the Old or the New Testament which is the exact equivalent of the theological idea of revelation, yet the divine revelation is the concern of the biblical message as a whole. A wide variety of expressions, facts, events, and processes in the Bible conveys something of the idea of revelation. These include theophanies, angelic messengers, dreams, oracles, visions, locutions, divine interventions in the processes of nature and history, and the words and deeds of the prophets. The culmination of God's self-manifestation, however, is in the person, life, passion, death, and resurrection of Jesus Christ and in the witness borne to him by the Holy Spirit, the apostles, and the believing community. The fixing of this primitive witness in written form gives to Holy Scripture itself the character of revelation.[6]

Nowhere else does the idea of revelation have the same radical meaning as when applied to the biblical message. Here, it cannot be expressed as an abstract idea, for that would place it within the possibility of human origin. Only through the historically "given" can its meaning ever be grasped; only in concrete events is made manifest that which otherwise would have remained absolutely hidden. And that which is revealed is not some supernatural knowledge or Absolute, but the personal God who is also Creator and Lord. He is not merely *a* subject, but Subject in the absolute sense. He is not merely *a* person, but Person in the absolute, unconditioned sense. And he is not merely concealed, but he is absolute mystery until he gives himself to be known. He himself, and not "something," is the real content of the biblical revelation. But in thus giving himself, he also makes known his nature and his will.[7]

Revelation in the biblical sense is a disclosure not only of God, but also of ourselves. To be without revelation is to be in absolute darkness or bondage, a condition which is both negative and personal in character. In the Fourth Gospel, it is expressed in the strongest of terms: one walks in darkness; he is lost. The Apostle Paul speaks of it as an alienation from God and as a being under the wrath of God. Man is not only a sinner; he *became* a sinner. He is not only blind; he *became* blind. He is not only alienated from God; he *became* alienated. Brunner understands this to mean that there has been a previous revelation apart from which man could not be a sinner. An original positive relation to God has been displaced by a negative relation.

There is a radical otherness about the biblical revelation. It is not merely an acquisition of new "knowledge" which one now possesses; rather it is a meeting of the Immutable with the mutable subject in which the latter is both transformed and finds true freedom in one who is now his Lord. Nor is one left in solitude with a new-found knowledge, for the knowledge of God with which revelation is concerned always creates community. Revelation, then, is inseparable from salvation; the history of the one is indeed the history of the other.

Again, revelation in the biblical sense is never concerned with that which could have been expected from any rational premise whatever. It discloses a radical form of love for which the New Testament writers use the word *agapē* rather than *eros*. This love is based upon the *will* to love and not upon any merit or value which is seen in its object. The amazing character of agape is expressed for all time by Paul who spoke of the love of Christ poured out unto death "while we were yet sinners" (Rom. 5:8). Revelation centers in the unique, unrepeatable, unconditionally personal event in which God himself is present with us as Redeemer. Attention is drawn to a decisive event at a specific time and place, to the sacrificial death of Christ on a cross. The reality of forgiveness, which is the focal point in revelation, hangs upon this "unconditioned unique event." And here, the mercy and holiness, the nature and the will of God, and his purpose for the world are unveiled to the eyes of faith.[8]

The work which Brunner himself considered his most definitive treatment of the fundamentally personal aspect of revelation is his *Truth as Encounter*, published near the midpoint of his career. The paradoxical title was deliberately chosen to express the biblical understanding of truth as a concrete "happening" rather than as a mere abstract concept. He set forth this work in an attempt to free the older concept of revelation from the intellectual misunderstanding imposed upon it by the Greek idea of truth. And ever afterward, he regarded the point of view amplified in this work as his most important contribution to the *theological* concept of knowledge.[9]

The significance of this insight for theology and the church was given formal expression in his later works—*Revelation and Reason*, and the three volumes of his *Dogmatics*. It was only after a lapse of twenty-five years that he undertook to set this idea "in its place within the context of a general *philosophical* problem of truth" (italics mine). This delay was deliberate in order to avoid the impression that he was "expounding a philosophy cut adrift from . . . the Christian faith" or possibly even presupposed by that faith. For Brunner, such a "subordination of theology to philosophy" would have been unthinkable. But he felt that he had now made his point; and in 1963, he published a new edition of *Truth as Encounter*, much enlarged for the purpose of making this adjustment.[10]

Opposing Views of Truth

At first sight, there appear to be two fundamentally opposing views of truth. On the one hand, modern man is preoccupied with the things of this world and with an immanental philosophy. Whatever cannot be fitted into the traditional categories of scientific objectivity or experiential subjectivity is for that reason suspect. There persists an unyielding demand for scientific proof, with a strong implication of the relativity of all truth. On the other hand, Christian theology and the church presume to speak of a revelation which *is* truth. Here is a claim to absolute truth, but one which can neither be proved by the intellect nor verified by experience. For modern man, moreover, this Christian claim to truth seems to have been seriously compromised by two glaring facts. In the first place, some of what the church long proclaimed as "revealed truth" has been conclusively demonstrated to have been in error. And in the second place, the claims of the church were bolstered for some fifteen hundred years by the stern authority of the state, which forbade as heresy all counter opinions.[11]

These considerations are accompanied by the further fact that the *nature* of revelation as a question in theology arose quite recently. Until post-Reformation thought, such discussion as was given to this subject usually centered in the relation between "natural" and "revealed" theology. And when attention was focused upon the meaning of revelation, it usually led to ecclesiastical theories of inspiration. This in turn led almost inevitably to the notion that divine revelation is the equivalent of a revealed *doctrine* or a book of divinely revealed doctrine. Against this time-honored view, Brunner contends that revelation is rather "God himself in his self-manifestation within history," that it is no less than "the whole of the divine activity for the salvation of the world." [12] He believes that this fundamental biblical view was briefly rediscovered during the period of the Reformation, but was soon lost in an inordinate desire to establish an authoritative safeguard for the renewed understanding of faith. An infallible Scripture was substituted for an infallible church. The subsequent breakdown of the notion of infallible Scripture under the impact of modern scientific and historical knowledge led to a collapse of the imposing structure of orthodox doctrine and to the enthronement of the "truth of reason." [13]

An attempt was made during the early phase of the Enlightenment [14] to set forth a rational view of the biblical revelation. This was soon abandoned, leaving reason alone as the basis of truth. Romantic idealism later attempted to broaden the concept of reason sufficiently to include within it the historical revelation, thus forming an impressive synthesis between Christianity and rationalistic philosophy. This apparent intellectual achievement was soon undermined by a "realistic-naturalistic reaction" against idealism. Meanwhile, a new school of thought arose within the Christian faith which sought to make revelation itself in its total historical reality the object of theological reflection. Instead of fixing attention upon supposed infallible verbal expressions, this school endeavored to get beyond the mere words of the Bible to the essential facts themselves. Thus for the first time in the history of Christianity, revelation was made "the primal and fundamental subject of theology." [15]

Reflecting upon these developments, Brunner undertook to reassess the whole concept of truth in the light of the presuppositions of reason and of the biblical message. His investigations led him to the conclusion that the entire history of Western philosophy and science had been in bondage to what he calls "the object-subject antithesis." Beginning with the ancient Greeks, it was first expressed as an antithesis between the world of the senses and the world of ideas. In post-Cartesian [16] philosophy, this Greek mode of thought was "sharpened into the antithesis of object and subject" and at the same time "expanded into a metaphysic of the mind." On the one side are the philosophies of the spirit or mind, where truth is understood as mental act. This is the perspective of idealism. And on the other side are the philosophies of nature, where truth is perceived as knowledge of that which is actually present to the senses. This is the perspective of realism.[17]

Brunner believes that neither idealism (which sees man merely as the knowing subject) nor realism (which sees him merely as the known object) gives us the truth about man. Proceeding on the assumption of an antithetical dichotomy between object and subject, they both fail to discern the essential unity of man; both fail to express his being as person, that is, as responsible being. The former sees the essence of his being as original, underived, and unconditioned, while the latter sees it as only an object present to the senses.[18]

The Theological Character of Truth

Brunner sees the problem of truth as primarily theological rather than philosophical. He begins with the premise that the Bible is the source and norm of all Christian theology and comes to the conclusion that there is a fundamental disparity between its understanding of truth and that which is determined by the object-subject antithesis. In the latter, the more precise and formal a concept becomes, the more fully is it apprehended and possessed. Hence, in the history of Christianity there has been, he contends, an inordinate disposition to objectify all aspects of the faith, including the understanding of truth. The Bible, however, contains no formal "doctrine of truth," just as it contains no formal doctrine of God, or of the Word of God, or of man. On the contrary, the more formal a theological concept becomes in its structure, the less can it be directly discovered in, or validated by the Bible. The Bible does not speak of God as he is in himself nor of man as he is in himself, but always of the two in relation one to the other. It speaks of the God who comes to man and of the man who has his being from God. In no sense is this a timeless, static relation arising from the world of ideas, in which case it might indeed be set forth in abstract doctrinal form. Rather, it is the relation of event (of happening) and can therefore be expressed only in narrative form. In this context, truth is understood as "personal encounter." [19]

In the phrase, "truth as encounter," Brunner brings together in one succinct expression the two centers of his theology, namely, the self-communicating God, and responsive man whom God has posited in freedom over against himself. God comes as the sovereign Lord who gives himself in love to man, and man responds in trustful obedience. The relationship which exists between God and man is here understood in terms of lordship and fellowship, which are central to the pivotal biblical concept of the Kingdom of God. God's will to lordship expresses his self-affirmation over against and in the creature, while his will to fellowship expresses his self-communication to the creature. Therefore, the decisive elements in the God-man relation are self-revelation and knowing. At the heart of this biblical view of truth is what Brunner refers to as "personal correspondence," [20] an expression which occurs again and again in his writing to indicate Person-to-person relations. He speaks of it as the basic category of Scripture. In the Bible, God is "never other than the God of man," and man is "never other than the man of God." In this context, truth, faith, and revelation are inseparable. Here, one not only *knows* the truth, but is *in* it.[21]

Brunner finds this idea of personal correspondence also at the center of the biblical understanding of faith. In biblical thought, the theologian is concerned with a theme which is absolutely unique, namely, the correlation of the Word of God and faith. While his thinking, like all thinking, is of necessity bound up with the object-subject correlation, his theme lies beyond it. Here, the discernment of truth is not at all a form of scientific thought, but is rather the response of faith to the God who meets one in the Word. Only as a believer may one perceive this theme. This is the case because what God communicates is not a "something," but rather himself. And likewise, instead of a pondering of "something," one is here confronted by a Person who speaks and discloses himself, thus taking over the role which thinking otherwise would take.

In perceiving this unique theme, one does not thereby gain disposal of it, as would be the case in knowing, thinking, or possessing something. Rather, one is himself thereby disposed or determined. And again, one is not left in his solitariness as would be the case if he were merely thinking in an I-orbit. He no longer has a monologue existence, for he is now confronted by another who says, "I am the Lord, thy God." He is addressed personally, and he gives a personal answer in the form of confession and prayer. In this personal exchange, the Word of God is not a formula to be believed, but it is directed address. Likewise, the response of faith is not a formulated credo, but it takes the form: "My Lord, and my God." In this purely personal encounter, the antithesis between object and subject has entirely disappeared. Or to state it another way, there is no longer an antithesis between "something true" and "knowledge of this truth," as in the general, rational understanding of truth. The essentials are now seen to be strictly limited to the Word of God and the obedience of faith, which issue in what the New Testament calls *agapē*—love that is willed.[22]

The opposite of this Word of God–faith encounter is what Brunner calls Credo-credo (Belief-belief) faith, which is belief in a formal confessional statement or creed. There is here no Thou-form of occurrence, but only an It-form of reflection, a belief in Belief. This Credo-credo faith may indeed be present without any semblance of agape.[23] There is therefore an abysmal difference between this nonpersonal relation and that which is central in the biblical category of personal correspondence. And yet, in giving himself (rather than doctrine) to us, God also says "something" to us, so that in some sense doctrine is contained even in the Word of God. His address in its direct and simplest form, "I am the Lord, thy God," is not comprehended apart from conceptualization. And likewise, the response of faith in prayer is expressive of a form of knowledge. In its most direct, simple, and personal form, "Our Father who art in heaven," there is a conceptual content.[24]

This means, then, that the personal encounter which is truth is also firmly linked with truth as doctrine. The more doctrine enables one to hear the address of God, however, the more does it actually point away from itself (i.e., from "something") to God himself. A principle of proximity is therefore operative which enables one to distinguish in some measure true doctrine from that which is heretical[25] and at the same time to avoid a legalistic understanding of doctrine. The presence of the Holy Spirit lends personal directness to doctrinal indirectness.[26] But the connection between truth as encounter and truth as doctrine must be clarified in order to avoid deviating toward either a false objectivism or a false subjectivism.

The Testing and Clarification of a Thesis

Brunner now moves on to examine and clarify his thesis with reference to the essential content of the biblical message. From the biblical perspective, each separate doctrine is regarded as valid in the measure that it actually points to God himself in his will to lordship and fellowship and to his act whereby he creates this lordship and this fellowship. With reference to the doctrine of the triune God, this means that we may not speculate about God as he is in himself, but speak only of the God who discloses himself in the historical revelation.[27] Likewise, with regard to God's will, we may not speculate concerning the eternal divine decrees, but must understand election and faith as correlative concepts, to be understood only in terms of personal correspondence.[28] And in reference to the doctrine of creation (especially in the New Testament understanding of the new creation), the idea of the *imago Dei* must no longer be understood as merely a human endowment marking man's original creation; it must now be seen as something that originates in the actual face-to-face encounter between this man and Christ. Instead of a static characteristic, the image of God in man is here seen as a concept of relation. Sin also must be understood as indicating an actual responsible relationship to God. Man's accountability for sin is the necessary correlative of the basic biblical idea that he is actually and genuinely "God's free counterpart." [29]

Continuing to examine the biblical understanding of truth and doctrine, Brunner applies his primary thesis to the central aspect of the Christian message, namely, the work and person of Christ. In the New Testament, faith is set forth in a variety of simple confessional forms which nevertheless indicate its nature with complete clarity. These forms may be subsumed in such expressions as "Jesus Christ, the Lord," or "Jesus Christ the Son of God," or "the Redeemer." Each of these phrases incorporates the essential elements of trust in and obedience to the Lord who is personally present. A decisive passage in the Prologue to the Fourth Gospel reads, "grace and truth came through Jesus Christ" (John 1:17). This passage is a clear reference to the event of the incarnation, which marks the coming into existence of grace and truth. Yet, the *work* of Christ is the pivotal point of the biblical revelation. The Scriptures are more concerned with the mystery of his work than with the secret of his person. Brunner believes that patristic theology in its Christological debates lost this insight.

Jesus Christ is to be seen as the *act* of God as well as the Word of God. The very name of the Redeemer (i.e., "Messiah") is a functional designation of his kingly role. Likewise, the priestly office of Christ emphasizes the unique doing and giving (the act) of God in the context of history. But the objective event "Christ" is never spoken of in Scripture apart from the response of faith. Indeed, Paul places the two on the same level when he uses the expressions "righteousness of God" and "righteousness of faith" interchangeably. Fellowship is not attained apart from personal correspondence. Brunner concludes this part of his argument, therefore, with the bold assertion, "*Faith is the truth.*" [30]

Other aspects of the biblical message are also examined in the light of Brunner's thesis of the demand for "personal correspondence," and in each case this demand is seen to be at the heart of the matter. The preaching of repentance calls for the surrender of the estranged will. Participation in the life of faith involves fellowship rather than union with God. Life in the community (the church) is understood in the personal rather than the institutional sense and as correlative to the Word of God. Finally, the ultimate goal for both the individual believer and the church is the consummation of the relation of personal correspondence. Then, the image of God in the new creation shall have been completed, thus bringing into effect the full realization of God's lordship and self-communication. Truth will then be realized as the perfect presence of God with his creation. The last word about truth is now seen to be fellowship rooted in God's self-communication.[31]

In the light of this development, Brunner believes that a more meaningful review may be undertaken regarding some aspects of the antithesis of objectivism and subjectivism in the history of Christianity. Both objectivism and subjectivism have marked every era of that history. Objectivism holds to the *first* basic fact of the relation of personal correspondence, namely, the prior act of God. It rightly observes that in that relation the Creator precedes the creation, the Word of God precedes the response of faith, God's act of atonement precedes justification, the witnessing church precedes individual faith, and the witness of Scripture precedes the illumination of the believer. Objectivism is an attempt to preserve the substance of this priority of the act of God. But in its zeal to safeguard the substance of the matter, its one-sidedness has generally led to torpidity on the part of the church.

Subjectivism, on the other hand, holds to the *second* basic fact of the relation of "personal correspondence," namely, the response from the side of man. It rightly emphasizes the fact that God's act in the free rule of the Spirit must be met by an equally free spiritual act from the side of man. But again, its one-sided emphasis inclines toward dissolution of that which is substantive in the faith. Of the two, subjectivism, where it occurs, more seriously jeopardizes the revelation. Yet, objectivism has always posed the greater ecclesiastical danger, because it is not so readily recognized as a danger.

There is within the church a never-ending struggle against false ecclesiasticism and false orthodoxy. Three forms of objectivism have been especially prominent in the history of the church, including the history of Protestantism. These are the objectivization of doctrine, of ecclesiastical office, and of the sacrament. Brunner takes these up one by one and shows how such objectivization violates the fundamental biblical understanding of personal correspondence.[32]

Objectivism in doctrine, according to Brunner, is the failure to distinguish between the Word of God and doctrine. Among Protestant churches, this false identification has been made most often with reference to the Scriptures. A doctrine of divine infallibility of Scripture has paralleled the Catholic doctrine of the infallibility of the pope. This ascription of infallibility to the text of Scripture is an application to the Bible of that ancient docetism which some of the early church Fathers applied to the person of Jesus Christ. In both cases, docetism marks an unbiblical reluctance to admit of a human element, which amounts to a denial of essential personal correspondence in the divine-human encounter. This rationalistic objectivization of the Word of God within Protestant orthodoxy marks what Brunner regards as a "false seeking for security," which fails to distinguish between "the fallible vessel and its divine infallible content."[33]

Closely related to the error inherent in this objectivization of the Word of God as infallible Scripture is another which disregards the variety of forms of theology in the Bible. It simply ignores the distinctions between a Pauline, a Johannine, and a Synoptic theology. No notice is taken of the difference between a priestly and a prophetic understanding of the Word of God, nor of the sometimes radically transformed character of the New Testament theology as compared with the Old. The reluctance of orthodoxy to recognize these distinctions grows out of a noble but misguided effort to protect and secure the words of Scripture. A hidden docetism here denies the genuine historicity of the divine revelation and seeks to interpose with a Platonic-like "timeless system of truth." The result is that a "timeless *doctrine* of salvation" is substituted for the biblical "*history* of salvation."

Another aspect of the false identification of the Word of God and doctrine is a failure to discern between the proclaiming and the didactic tasks of the church. Proclamation, which is the primary commission of the church, is essentially personal in character and faith awakening in purpose. It initiates faith, and a believing congregation is thereby gathered. Doctrine, on the other hand, serves its rightful role when it strengthens existing faith and deepens knowledge of that faith. An overvaluation of doctrine, relying as it does on logic, can be actually damaging when it becomes disproportionate to the actual measure of faith which is present. Confusion at this point often leads to unprofitable doctrinal disputes.[34]

Objectivism in the understanding of the sacraments has also done serious violence to the biblical understanding of personal correspondence in the divine-human encounter. Brunner illustrates the problem here with a critical discussion of baptism. He finds that in those biblical passages where baptism is dealt with in a didactic context, it is a two-sided affair, representing an initial sovereign act of grace on the part of God and a corresponding act of receiving and confessing on the part of the recipient. One allows himself thereby to be drawn into the death of Christ and manifests his own personal faith in the reality of the resurrection life. Catholic doctrine and practice, however, with its view of baptism as an *opus operatum,* departed entirely from the biblical understanding of the matter. Nothing here would suggest that the one receiving baptism is in any sense a responding subject. In dire circumstances, even the fetus in the womb of its mother may be the recipient of baptism.

In opposition to this thoroughgoing objectivism, the Reformation principle of *nullum sacramentum sine fide* affirmed that there is no sacrament apart from faith. Brunner holds that this valid insight was immediately vitiated, however, both in Lutheranism and in the Reformed wing of the Reformation, by the retention of infant baptism. Orthodox Lutheranism maintains that faith is somehow present in the infant,[35] and Reformed theology holds that a proxy covenant-faith in the parents and witnesses suffices meanwhile for the baptism of the infant. In both cases, genuine personal correspondence is seriously disturbed if not completely nullified. Uneasiness at this point led to the establishment of a subsequent rite of confirmation in which the missing element of response was added. Brunner sees this as in effect a dividing of the New Testament act of baptism into two parts. He charges that this objectivistic outlook in contemporary theology is so prevalent that the problem here goes unnoticed. He sees the contemporary practice of infant baptism as nothing short of "scandalous." It has led to an inclusion, in a sort of "people's church," of many persons who at heart do not wish to confess Christ as Lord. To the extent that this objectivization occurs, the concept of the church is transformed from that of a personal to that of an institutional entity. Thus despoiled of personal correspondence, the church ceases to be understood as a holy communion and is seen as a sacred institution.[36]

Finally, objectivism in the understanding of ecclesiastical office has done immeasurable violence to the biblical understanding of the nature of the church and its ministry. The New Testament does in fact recognize a variety of functional roles in the church, but they are wholly spiritual in character and control. Nowhere is there to be found an alien ecclesiastical law by which such roles are appointed and regulated. There is always a specific correlation between offices and *charismata* (or spiritual gifts). The office-bearer performs his function only in the actuality of his *charisma.*

From the second century onward, the church sought to protect itself from hostile forces without and within by means of the establishment of the historic episcopate. But this solution, as necessary as it may have been under the circumstances, also brought about a transformation in the understanding of the very reality it sought to protect. The church was now seen as an objective reality, existing, so to speak, in its own right. Within its life was conceived to be an authoritative ministry dispensing valid sacraments for the salvation of another segment of believers from whom the former were qualitatively separated by means of ordination.

Brunner believes that in seeking to rectify this situation, the Reformation leaders faltered halfway between Catholicism and the church order of the New Testament. He points out that even within Protestantism, the prophetic-personal Word of God has too often been displaced by "pure doctrine," and that spiritual qualifications for ministry have too often been displaced by canonical qualifications for office. Brunner now reaches the conclusion that objectivization was already assured in the key words of the Reformation whereby the church was identified with the right preaching of the Word (i.e., pure doctrine) and with the right administration of the sacraments (i.e., according to correct form). This formula does not allow for the freedom of the living Word nor for the fact that the church, the ecclesia, has not only its origin, but also its continued existence in the reality of the call of God and the response of faith. This one-sided objectivism, moreover, has militated against the church's understanding itself as a missionary reality in the world.[37]

THE PROBLEM OF NATURAL THEOLOGY

A further matter vitally related to Brunner's understanding of revelation and reason is his view of natural theology. His thought regarding this subject is set forth in an article entitled "Nature and Grace," [38] which appeared in 1934 as his principal contribution to the famous controversy between himself and Karl Barth. He begins by calling appreciative attention to Barth's contributions to theology and to those matters which the two of them hold in common. Among the latter, special mention is made of the following: the fact that Holy Scripture alone is regarded as the source and norm of the church's proclamation; that this proclamation is understood as a message centering alone in the free and sovereign grace of God who comes with salvation to enslaved man; that salvation is offered in the cross of Christ; that the Holy Spirit enables the assimilation of the word of the cross; and that Christian action on the part of the church and of the individual believer is always under the primary command of God. Brunner now briefly outlines six conclusions which Barth draws from these premises, all of which are so formulated as to reject any idea of natural theology.

In opposition to Barth's conclusions, Brunner poses six countertheses of his own, which indicate his attempted solution of the then much debated question as to the continuity or discontinuity between the biblical revelation and all claims based on general revelation. The essence of his argument is as follows. First, in discussing the original image of God in man in relation to the fall, he holds that it must be seen under two aspects, the one formal and the other material. The *formal* aspect of this concept is that which indicates man's humanness, his superiority within the creation, his special relation to God, his responsibility. This aspect was never lost. Even as a sinner, man is responsible before God. The *material* aspect, on the other hand, was utterly lost. Man is sinful and rebellious to the very core of his being. He is still a responsive person, but his response has become antipersonal. The divine purpose of personal correlation is broken.

Brunner's second thesis is that the world is God's creation and the scene of his continued activity. As such, it bears something of his imprint upon it. Revelation in some measure is therefore present in nature, in the human conscience, and in history. His third thesis is that God is still present even to fallen man by means of "preserving grace," as is manifest in his provision for natural and historical life and sustenance. A fourth thesis is that there are divine ordinances of nature which belong to the sphere of divine preservation rather than to that of redemption. These ordinances are discovered only in faith; yet they employ natural impulse and reason. They provide constancy in social and historical life and as such are basic to all ethical problems. These ordinances, however, are of differing levels of dignity. Monogamous marriage, for example, is understood as an "ordinance of creation, whereas the State is seen as an ordinance of preservation," made necessary because of sin.

A fifth thesis is that since only human subjects can receive the Word of God and the Holy Spirit, there is within even sinful man a "point of contact" for God's grace of redemption. Brunner understands this point of contact as the formal responsive aspect of the image of God which remains intact even in man's sinful rebellion and assures thc possibility of his being addressed. Only a responsive being can be addressed; and only one addressed can be responsible. The possibility of sin does not arise apart from the fact that the responsive creature is in fact addressed. But this carries the presupposition that natural man in some measure knows that he is a sinner, however blurred this knowledge may be. Only so may he discern the divine message of grace. It carries the further presupposition that in some measure he knows God, however imperfect that knowledge may be. Only in this consciousness of God is there the possibility of his receiving the divine Word. And finally, a sixth thesis is that self-consciousness is preserved in the act of faith because the personal God meets man only in a personal way. This is why the new creation may be understood only in terms of restoration.[39]

III. The Christian Doctrine of God

One's understanding of God and the proper relation to him is determinative for every other doctrinal concern. As already indicated, the whole of Brunner's theology is built within the framework of the self-representation of God. The seriousness with which he takes the person, the nature, and the will of God is one of the distinctive features of his theological system. His view of God might indeed be constructed satisfactorily from that which is expressed in his treatment of other cardinal doctrines of the Christian faith. Yet, there are certain writings in which he gives special attention to this subject. His most extensive work on this theme is *The Christian Doctrine of God*, which is the first volume of his *Dogmatics*. Other volumes include individual chapters which deal with some aspect of the doctrine of God. Among these are *The Scandal of Christianity*, *God and Man*, *Our Faith*, and *I Believe in the Living God*.[1]

The title which Brunner gives to this division of his comprehensive exposition in the *Dogmatics* reads, "The Eternal Foundation of the Divine Self-communication." Here is already suggested the point of view from which he approaches the doctrine of God. In this work, he centers attention upon the nature of God and his eternal will, neither of which may be known apart from his own self-disclosure.

In his treatment of the doctrine of God, Brunner finds it necessary from the outset to identify the deity of whom he speaks.

This is made necessary, he believes, because philosophy, too, would speak confidently and in its own right concerning this subject. Philosophy, of course, has taken many forms and has varied radically in its presuppositions, methodology, and language. But whatever its form, the fundamental feature is always its empirical basis. When the philosopher, as philosopher, attempts to scale the lofty heights from the conditioned to the unconditioned and to speak of ultimate reality, there appear to be three possible ways open to him. He may take the approach of *idealism* (which marks the way from the subject), or that of *realism* (which marks the way from the object), or he may adopt some form of the doctrine of *identity* (which is believed to transcend the antithesis between subject and object). In any case, he simply adopts the language of religion and speaks of the end result as "God."

Realism begins with the facts of experience, somewhat from the point of view of a spectator, and attempts to follow those lines in the world of experience which appear to converge toward a common point beyond the range of the empirical. Making use of such concepts as causality and analogy, it seeks an ultimate point of unity in the laws of nature, which it does not hesitate to call "God." Idealism, on the other hand, begins with the self, not as a mere spectator, but as potential master. Instead of searching for causes in the laws of nature, it seeks the ground of reality and the meaning of all things in the depths of that spirit in which the philosopher himself participates. Here alone, it is held, is the absolute finally disclosed. The philosophy of identity begins with a recognition of the antithesis between object and subject, but holds that underneath that antithesis is a hidden unity which embraces both. This unity cannot be known positively, but it is believed to be indicated through a process of negations. It discloses itself, not to the intellect, but to feeling or intuition. The philosopher of identity speaks of this unity as "God" and the consciousness of this unity as "religion." [2]

The tenacity of these three speculative possibilities is apparent in the fact that they recur again and again in the history of thought with something akin to an inner necessity. Yet, they continually appear side by side and in mutual opposition. Each appears to exist in the main as counterpoint to false elements in the other two. Each represents a monistic system in which it is simply assumed that one's own thought is able to penetrate to the very ground and unity of all things. In the final analysis, one assumes continuity between the thinking self and that ultimate reality which he calls "God." Again, each system is only a monologue of the solitary thinker with himself, in which he alone poses the questions and answers them. No word from beyond the thinking self is either sought or permitted.

The situation is really no different, Brunner believes when the solitary thinker turns philosopher of history and clothes his abstract ideas in flesh and blood. He is still engaged in a monologue. The only God he perceives is that which speaks out of, and is identical with, the depths of his own spirit. In short, this God exists as an idea, a philosophical concept which is arrived at by means of a system. This is not the personal Creator-God of biblical thought who breaks into one's solitude and speaks an authoritative word *to* him.[3]

The biblical understanding of God is radically different from that of any philosophical concept whatsoever. It never rests upon a metaphysical foundation, nor is it the product of a rational system. Here, God is not conceived of as an idea. He is rather apprehended in his own revelation of himself in history. It is not history which reveals God, but God who reveals himself in history. He remains altogether hidden and unknown until he reveals himself, when and where he wills. In his revelation, it is not merely *something* which God gives, but it is himself and his will that are imparted. This is the whole point of the biblical witness.

To speak of the hidden God who remains absolute mystery until he reveals himself, is to acknowledge him as Lord. Only the biblical God of revelation is beyond the grasp of human thought. All else can be fitted into a system over which the thinker exercises dominion. For that very reason, the God of the philosophers can never be Lord. Where God is Lord, the thinker and his whole rational system are brought under the dominion of that one who is so revealed. God, the Lord, cannot be made an object; he is always Subject. In this context, even knowledge itself is a radically different kind of knowing. Rather than achieving mastery over all things by means of an autonomous system, one's very knowing becomes an act of obedience.[4]

The knowledge of God as Lord marks a transformation in one's very existence. This, Brunner argues, is not a transformation by natural process; it has rather the character of decision and abdication. The knowledge of God as Lord is always accompanied by the knowledge of sin. But the idea of sin is just that which is rejected by every monistic system of thought, for an acknowledgment of the reality of sin would in the end be destructive of the system itself. Where God is not received as Lord, one is bound either to ignore sin or to interpret it in terms of some negative magnitude such as error, weakness, imperfection, ignorance, or the like.

Further, Brunner believes that the fact of evil in the world renders every religious thought-system as such a theodicy—a justification of that world from the standpoint of God. Speculative philosophy assumes that all contradictions in the world can in fact be ultimately resolved by the powers of thought. In biblical faith, however, these contradictions are seen to be very real and therefore to be resolved only through God's act of redemption. For that reason, where philosophy employs some form of theodicy, the Bible makes use of eschatology. Brunner holds that one must choose between theodicy and eschatology, that he cannot have both.[5]

Again, knowledge of God as Lord in the biblical sense of that word always involves decision, especially when he is acknowledged as one's own Lord. But decision is alien to the philosophical system, for in the latter one simply has to recognize an essential unity which already exists between the thinker and God. Nothing is left to decide concerning that essential relationship; it is there from the beginning. Brunner holds, however, that to know God as one's Lord, and to decide for and acknowledge him as such are one and the same thing. And to know him thus as Lord is to have one's whole existence determined by him.[6]

That which most clearly distinguishes the self-revealed God of Christian faith from the God of speculative thought, however, lies in the realm of the personal. What God is in himself and what he is in relation to his creatures can only be received; it cannot be thought. But in revealing himself to knowledge, he also imparts himself in love. And in so doing, he speaks the vital word of forgiveness, which only the Lord can speak. In this meeting of the divine "Thou" and the human "I" is seen the truly personal event of one's life. The singularity of the appearance of God in Christ is met by the response of faith, which involves the supreme decision of one's life. And where faith is introduced (this response which also has its source in God), all speculative thought is at an end. The continuity of self with Self in monologue is now seen to be an impossibility. As a man of faith, the thinker now distinguishes between his thought and faith itself. God ceases to be the mere object of thought, for faith is not one's knowing of God so much as it is a being known of God and an assurance that one is so known. In faith, the thinker adopts the attitude of the listening servant and lets God say who he is. It is as the listening servant that Brunner now undertakes to speak of the God who reveals himself.[7]

THE NATURE OF GOD

In approaching this subject, Brunner assumes that one may not know what God is in himself apart from special revelation. Because he dwells in unfathomable mystery, only God himself can tell us who he is. Brunner finds it highly significant therefore that at the center of the biblical witness is the disclosure of the *name* of God. At an early stage in the history of the Old Testament, the proper name Yahweh was used to distinguish the God of Israel from the gods of other nations. But even after the need for such a distinction had passed, the concept of the "name of the Lord" remained central to the biblical message. It was still a prominent feature of both the teaching and the praying of Jesus. The first petition of his model prayer was "Hallowed be thy name" (Matt. 6:9). And in his extended prayer in the Fourth Gospel, he declared, "I manifested thy name unto the men whom thou gavest me out of the world" (John 17:6). In this same prayer he petitioned, "Holy Father, keep them in thy name" (John 17:11).[8]

Brunner holds that the whole meaning of the biblical doctrine of God is contained in its understanding of the "name" of God and the manifestation of that name. The name of God is used in its biblical context to designate that which is peculiar to himself. It suggests that God is person, that he alone can name himself, and therefore that he is not an object of thought. In communicating his name, he in fact gives himself away and makes possible a covenant relationship. But also, in giving his name, he summons us to make use of that name in calling upon him. And again, this giving of his name, and the necessity from our side for his doing so, means the end of man's self-sufficient isolation in the quest for truth.[9]

In giving his name, God does not simply define for us his nature, but rather reveals himself as Lord. This insight was probably first indicated by the translators of the Septuagint who rendered the name "Yahweh" with the title "Lord"—thus: "I am the Lord, thy God" (Exod. 20:2). The force of this rendering is particularly strong in the passage "I, even I, am Jehovah [i.e., the Lord]; and beside me there is no saviour" (Isa. 43:11). The uniqueness and sovereignty of God became increasingly manifest in the historical character of his revelation. It is he who summons us unequivocally to "hear" what he would say, and he alone to whom we are bidden to turn for help. He is absolute Lord. Brunner insists that this is the point from which dogmatic reflection must begin and to which it must return again and again. It must not be undertaken from the neutral position of a mere definition of the Godhead.

God, the Lord, comes to us as person (as Subject) in the absolute sense. He speaks and acts, and in so doing, reveals both himself and his will. As divine and sovereign majesty, he claims us unconditionally for himself. For this reason, we know him first as Lord, and only then as Creator—though in knowing the former, we also know the latter. As Lord, he is also Creator and Revealer. The highest manifestation of God's sovereign freedom is seen where he stands above his own law and forgives the sinner. Where God has revealed himself in such a manner, there is no room for an intrusion of that speculative thought which belongs to natural theology and which would presume to begin with "proofs" of the existence of God. The Christian doctrine of the God of faith belongs to a radically different order of knowing and theologizing.[10]

Intimately related to the idea of the sovereignty of God, Brunner holds, is that of his holiness. The Old Testament in its entirety is a revelation of the holy God; and though the emphasis upon holiness is somewhat diminished in the New Testament, it is everywhere presumed. Nowhere is it so impressive as in the mode of address employed by Jesus, "Holy Father, keep them in thy name" (John 17:11), or in the address prescribed in the model prayer, "Hallowed be thy name" (Matt. 6:9). From the objective point of view, a recognition of the holy is the highest response of religious discernment. Likewise, from the subjective point of view, the worship of the holy God is the supreme response of religious faith. Whereas in non-Christian religions, the idea of the holy may be attached indiscriminately to various objects, at least in its highest manifestation in the biblical revelation, it is ascribed to the very nature of God.

Holiness, in the biblical sense of that term, is that which distinguishes the transcendent God from all else—it is that which marks him as "Wholly Other." It is his holiness which renders it impossible to compare him with any nature-god whatsoever, and it is this which lies behind the commandment forbidding the worship of graven images. But this aspect of his nature is not to be seen as a static quality. It is an active expression of his will as the "jealous God" (Exod. 20:5) who will not give his glory to another (Isa. 42:8). It is a positive assertion that he alone is God. The positive and the negative sides of this aspect of his being are expressed respectively in the idea of the glory of God and that of his wrath.

God wills that "the whole earth be filled with his glory" (Ps. 72:19). This is fundamental to the biblical idea of revelation. He wills to be recognized as the God he is. His glory, expressive of both his sovereignty and his revelation, attains its end only as it is mirrored in the hearts of believers. But this expansive and inclusive movement of the divine will represents only one aspect of the holiness of God. Parallel to it is another movement of that will which at first sight appears to contradict the first and to indicate "withdrawal and exclusion." This is the wrath of God, which resists all that opposes his will.

In and of himself, only God is holy. But in a secondary sense, all that he claims and sets apart for himself is holy, for that which he separates for his own peculiar possession, he also hallows. At an early stage in the witness of the Old Testament, the idea of the holy was nonethical; God was understood as hallowing not only persons, but animals, various objects, places, and even times and seasons. By the time of the eighth- and seventh-century prophets, this nonethical idea of holiness was disappearing. It had entirely disappeared by the time of the New Testament. Here, that which is holy has taken on the character of the morally good; and it is good simply because it conforms to the will of God, which is "the foundation of all true morality." Sainthood is therefore willing and loving obedience to his will.[11]

Whereas in the Old Testament, the pivotal idea is that of the holiness of God, in the New Testament it is that of his love. Yet, in the latter it is the love of the *holy* God which predominates; and conversely, it is the holiness of the God who *loves* which is assumed. Therefore, in the Christian idea of God, his holiness and his love are inseparable. The message that God is love, however, is unique among the religions of mankind, and it is contrary to every rational system of thought. The God of the biblical revelation, and he alone, condescends to man in grace and mercy.

Already in the Old Testament in the thought of Hosea and Jeremiah, and in the Book of Deuteronomy, the witness to God's unmerited love is firmly portrayed. It is only in the gospel of the New Testament, however, that this love becomes the dominant theme. Only in the light of the mission of Jesus is it possible to assert, "God is love" (1 John 4:8, 16). Love is not simply a divine attribute, nor is it a quality which might be shared by others. It is rather the very *nature* of God. Therefore, it can be said, "he that abideth in love abideth in God" (1 John 4:16). This means, of course, that we cannot know what love is apart from what is given in revelation. Here, it is seen as the very self-giving of the holy God.

In non-Christian thought, the idea of love (expressed in Greek usage by the term *eros*) signifies an attraction to that which has value and worth. Here, love is simply evoked by that which is its object, whether it be the love between man and woman, the love of country, the love of beauty or friendship, or whatever may be prized for its own value. The love of God (the *agapē* of the New Testament), however, is unmotivated; it is poured out freely and lavishly upon the worthless, the degraded, and the unfaithful. God's love does not find expression in the bestowal of *something*, but in the giving of his very self. Such incomprehensible love can arise only within his own will and can be known only through revelation. This love and this revelation are the two elements in the self-communication of God.

Thus far, it has been seen that there is a necessary connection between *holiness* and revelation and between *love* and revelation. Brunner now raises the question as to the relation between love and holiness in the nature of the God who reveals himself. At first sight, they appear to oppose each other. Holiness is that aspect of the will of God which sets him apart, asserting his glory and sovereignty. Love is that aspect of his will which breaks through every barrier between God and man and brings him near. It is only from the point of view of sinful man that holiness and love could be seen as in opposition one to the other. In reality, they are inseparable; each merges into and completes the other. Nowhere is the unity of the two in the nature of God more manifest than in the prayer of Jesus: "Holy Father, keep them in thy name which thou hast given me, that they may be one, even as we are . . . that the world may know that thou didst send me, and lovedst them, even as thou lovedst me" (John 17:11, 23). This entire prayer revolves around the themes of holiness, glory, love, and communion.[12]

Brunner sees that the holy God whose eternal nature is love, is also the self-communicating God who revealed himself in Jesus Christ. This unity of his nature and of his revelation already brings before us that mystery of his being which the church has sought to express in its doctrine of the Trinity.[13] Historically, the dogma of the Trinity has been regarded as the most distinctive element in the Christian view of God, and also the most problematic. It was never, as such, a part of the apostolic witness, and at no time has it been accepted by Christians as a whole. Yet, since the fourth century, the mainstream of Christian tradition has looked upon it as central to both its theology and its faith. Brunner holds that the ecclesiastical dogma of the Trinity was not a part of the biblical proclamation and therefore does not belong to the church's *message*. It is rather a theological doctrine which was formulated for the defense of the central aspect of the Christian faith. It belongs, therefore, to the sphere of theological *reflection* whereby the church tests its message in the light of that Word which God has given to it.

The doctrine of the Triune God arises out of the simple and informal witness to him in the New Testament. All that belongs to the gospel (whether Kingdom of God, incarnation, atonement, redemption, or final consummation) revolves around three divine names: the Father, the Son, and the Holy Spirit. The God who gives his name to be known as the Father is revealed in the Son; and both Father and Son are given to the church through the Holy Spirit. It was inevitable, therefore, that the question should arise sooner or later as to the relation between these three names.[14]

Brunner points out, therefore, that the New Testament has no interest in the Trinity as a problem of thought. It sets forth a view of Jesus as the giver and revealer of God's love. As the revelation of God, he differs from the one who is revealed; yet as the revealer of this God, he is identical with him. This objective, historical revelation, this distinction in unity between the revealer and the revealed made subjective to us in the Holy Spirit, is what is meant by the Trinity of God. And this is the extent of the interest which the New Testament has in the subject. The theoretical questions as to how the three are one and as to their relations one to the other lie not only in mystery, but are outside biblical concern. Brunner holds that it is that which stands revealed, and not the mystery of the Trinity, which is the proper object of our adoration and praise. The dogma of the Trinity can be regarded as trustworthy only insofar as it is faithful to the historical center of revelation and is not deflected to a speculative interest in the eternal background.[15]

Brunner now turns his attention to a consideration of the traditional but problematic question of the divine attributes. He holds that on the basis of revelation we not only may, but must, speak positively regarding God's holiness, his sovereign freedom, his love, and his self-sufficiency. These all have to do with what he is in himself. All other attributes which have been ascribed to God have meaning only as they indicate his nature in regard to particular aspects of his created order. Brunner believes, however, that in the development of the doctrine of the divine attributes, there has been an intrusion of alien and distorting elements into Christian thought from the side of speculative philosophy.[16] This, he warns, makes it imperative that the theologian remain firmly grounded in biblical thought while dealing with this question.

In keeping with the truth already indicated that God gives

himself to be known first as Lord, the Bible bears witness to him as almighty. It does so, however, only in a *relational* context and never as an expression of what he is in himself. He is almighty in relation to nature and the laws of nature. Brunner points out that to speak of God simply as "the Almighty" is to employ an abstraction. It is to define him as pure "Being," whereas in reality his almightiness (his omnipotence) is inseparable from his holiness and his love.[17]

In like manner, the Bible witnesses to the divine immanence (the presence of God) in the created order. But when speculative metaphysical thought employs the term, "omnipresence," it does so almost inevitably in terms of pantheism.[18] So to speak is to lose the intensive, qualitative, and nonspatial sense in which God comes to us—and in coming, may yet be spoken of as "near" or "far" from us.

Again, the Bible testifies to the fact that God "knows" man; but this is always represented as a personal and interested form of knowing. When the Bible says that God knows a man, it means that he loves him and elects him and extends to him his gracious call. Here, there is an indissoluble connection between divine knowing, creating, loving, and choosing. Speculative thought, on the other hand, speaks of "omniscience," which Brunner finds to be a radically different kind of knowing. It implies on the one hand that God knows everything. And on the other hand, it suggests an undifferentiated, objective, and therefore neutral kind of knowing, which could be of no value to man.[19]

In biblical thought, moreover, the eternity of God is expressive of his unchangeableness and of his sovereignty. In that sovereign freedom, he stands above time as its Creator and Lord, yet enters purposefully into time. By contrast, Brunner argues, speculative thought tends to understand eternity as simply timelessness. Here, time has no relation to the realm of ideas and therefore no share in the truth. And because it has no interest in time as such, speculative philosophy has no regard for history either. The biblical God, on the other hand, is known only through his acts in history.[20]

His entering into time as the living Lord (in contradistinction to the God of speculative thought) is that which manifests his *faithfulness*—the holding fast to his purpose of creation in spite of man's sinfulness. It was this faithfulness and long-suffering of the holy and loving God which comprised the substance of the joyful tidings of prophets and apostles. A closely related idea is that of the *righteousness* of God, which likewise indicates the constancy of his will in the light of his avowed purpose for his people. This term is an inexact rendering of two key biblical words. The first is the Hebrew word *ts'daga,* which can be applied to God in the sense just indicated. It can also be applied to the man who is in covenant relation with God. The second biblical word which is rendered by the term "righteousness" is the Pauline expression *dikaiosunē.* As it is used in the Epistle to the Romans, this word is a fulfillment of the meaning of the Old Testament word *ts'daga.* In this Pauline context, it is used to express the serious, but inconceivable blending of God's holiness and his love in the cross of Christ.[21]

Again, there is a *wisdom* of God which is set forth in his created order and which is in some sense accessible to reason. In the New Testament, however, the divine wisdom is expressed more frequently in relation to God's sovereign control of events in history. Here, everything that happens is regarded as a means of his wisdom—even those things which appear contradictory to his revealed purpose. The supreme example of this display of divine wisdom is in that event which appeals to reason as the "folly" of the cross (1 Cor. 1:18 ff.). Such wisdom is accessible only to that faith which is based upon the Christian revelation.[22]

Finally, something must be said about the *glory* of God. This mysterious, biblical word expresses an idea which is almost incomprehensible in meaning. It is not a concept descriptive of God as he is in himself; nor is it an attribute expressive of his relation to some aspect of the created order. It is both objective and subjective in character. It designates for the eye of faith both the being and the presence of God in the fullness of his revelation and the realization of his divine sovereignty. The glory of God is at once his revealed nature, his accomplished will, and his realized presence.[23]

THE WILL OF GOD

Brunner finds the eternal will of God (the same as the divine nature) to be hidden in mystery, except insofar as it is self-revealed. And furthermore, he believes that the biblical witness decidedly directs our attention away from the eternal background, to the historical revelation. On the other hand, he is aware that it is the biblical message of *election* which renders this subject unavoidable, for it points to an origin and an end in the Word of God, beyond the reaches of history.[24]

Brunner also believes that the biblical idea of election has often been vitiated by attempts to pry into the mystery of God and thereupon to formulate a binding doctrine of predestination in terms of eternal divine decrees. The effect of this rational process has been not only the undermining of human dignity and responsibility, but also a disparagement of God's love. In the New Testament, faith is never directed toward a general statement of belief in the form of a doctrine. It is always a result of personal encounter with God in Christ, who though unique and unfathomable, is nevertheless God in action. Brunner interprets election, therefore, as both granted and received in the historical and inseparable "Act-Word" of the living God. It is understood as indeed a call from eternity; but the eye of faith remains firmly fixed upon the historical center where alone is the possibility of responsible human decision and action.[25]

A misunderstanding of the biblical idea of election may lead in several different directions, with dire consequences for true personhood. As Brunner points out, it may lead to universalism, in which no room is left for a meaningful decision in faith. It may result in a psychological notion of passivity in which there is only a causal relation between God and man and faith exists only as a divine effect. Or again, election may be understood in terms of a pretemporal divine decision regarding man. In its ultimate form, this last theological deviation from biblical teaching results in the doctrine of "double predestination," in which by divine decree, each man's eternal destiny is understood as having been irrevocably determined before the creation of the world. In spite of the fact that this rigid view has been especially associated with his own Reformed tradition in history, Brunner rejects it as having no basis in Scripture.[26]

IV. The Christian Doctrine of Man

Brunner regarded the doctrine of man as "the cardinal point" of his theology.[1] His Christian anthropology is never really concealed in any of his writings, but particular attention is devoted to various aspects of it in a number of special monographs and finally in his *Dogmatics*. The more significant of his writings on this subject are the following, arranged in chronological order: *God and Man; The Divine Imperative; Man in Revolt; The Letter to the Romans; Justice and the Social Order; Christianity and Civilization; The Word of God and Modern Man;* and *The Christian Doctrine of Creation and Redemption.* A comprehensive treatment of his anthropology would include four principal divisions: man before God, man in society, man and civilization, and man in the modern world. Limitations of space dictate, however, that only the first two may here be undertaken.

MAN BEFORE GOD

Presuppositions of the Christian Doctrine of Man

Brunner's doctrine of man is constructed upon certain fundamental presuppositions. In the first place, he believes that man must be understood in the light of a realm from beyond himself. From the Christian perspective, this "beyond" is inseparable from the living, personal God who gives himself to be known, and in so doing helps man also to know himself. In the second place, this doctrine presupposes the truths of the Christian revelation, yet without abandoning or contradicting that which is accessible to experience. In the third place, the Word of God is here regarded not only as the source of knowledge of man in his essential being, but also as the very ground of his being.

Closely related to the above presuppositions is a fourth, namely, that there is continuity in the creative and redemptive activity of God. Only in the latter can man really know the former. But for Brunner, redemption is far more than the mere restoration of the creation. Man, in spite of his perversion, remains in the creative hands of his God, the goal of whose continuing work has its eternal consummation in the divine plan disclosed in Jesus Christ.

A fifth and final presupposition is that every man is in some measure conscious of the twofold character of human existence. He is aware of both the glory and the misery of that existence. On the one hand, he knows that something in his very constitution distinguishes him from the rest of creation. But on the other hand, he is in some measure aware of a deep-rooted contradiction at the very core of his being.[2]

In the light of these presuppositions, Brunner's understanding of man before God is brought to focus upon three constitutive elements: the origin of man; the contradiction in man; and the resultant conflict between the two. In combination, these elements set the Christian doctrine of man apart from all other anthropologies.

Man in His Origin

In his discussion of the origin of man, Brunner employs what he regards as a parabolic expression from the creation narrative in the Book of Genesis. The phrase in question declares that man has been created "in the image of God," an expression which Brunner cites as the *imago Dei.* He finds this linguistic figure to be used only a very few times in the whole of the Bible and believes that its full meaning is perceived only in the light of the revelation given in Christ.[3]

The idea of the image of God in the Old Testament, Brunner believes, is to be understood in the "formal" or structural sense of that term. In that context, the emphasis is upon the being of man as subject, as free, and as having dominion in the world. It is this which constitutes his specifically *human* quality and at the same time renders him responsible before God.[4] The New Testament presupposes this indestructible formal aspect, but its emphasis is upon the "material" aspect of man's nature. Here, "the image of God" receives further illumination in various allusions to man's sonship, his likeness to Christ, and his relation to the Word of God. From this perspective, the idea of the image of God is no longer confined to a rigid, structural interpretation, but is understood as existence in the Word of God through faith. Brunner regards this insight as basic to his whole theology.

The New Testament expands the Old Testament insight that man is answerable to his Creator in a manner of life which renders honor, reverence, and grateful love. But it makes unmistakably clear the fact that man has given a tragically different answer than that which was divinely appointed him. It also proclaims another gracious act of God in which man's false answer has been reversed. The New Testament, therefore, can represent the material aspect of the image of God in man as having been wholly lost, but also as having been fully restored through the reconciling and redemptive work of Jesus Christ. Once more, then, man is represented as receiving the primal Word of God at the very core of his being. And therein, he has his existence.[5]

The meaning of the image of God in man is gained, Brunner contends, through reflection upon what is given to us in Jesus Christ. It may not be perceived by speculation as to its use in the creation narrative. It was at this point, he believes, that the ecclesiastical development of this doctrine went astray in the theology of the early Christian centuries. From Irenaeus to Augustine, theologians wrestled with the meaning of the phrase in Genesis 1:26, "in our image, after our likeness." Failing to recognize this expression as an instance of Hebrew parallelism, they tended to interpret the phrase "after our likeness" as indicating an addition to man's essential humanity which they understood as represented in the phrase "in our image." On this premise, they were inclined to understand man's communion with God as something added to his humanity. In the light of Christ, however, such communion is revealed to be the very essence of that humanity. The point here is that man bears a personal, not a structural, relation to God.

Taking the biblical phrase in question as only a parable, and thus bearing a concealed meaning, Brunner understands the term *image* in the sense of a reflection of something outside of man himself. Thus, it has meaning only as it points away from oneself (or any self-consisting substance in oneself) and back to the very ground of one's existence. This is to say in effect (and in opposition to all rational thought) that man has no intrinsic worth in himself, but only in the primal Word of God through which he came into being and by which he continues to exist. This means also that whereas man is created in and for the Word of God, he must be always actively receiving that Word, for he remains in the creative hands of his God. Of all the works of God, man remains the unfinished creation. He is posited over against God, with the inescapable necessity of engaging in responsive and responsible decision through which he either affirms or rejects that primal Word in which alone he may have true human existence. In the final analysis, therefore, it is not merely a question of an image, or even of a reflection, but rather of a Word and an answer. What this means is clearly perceived when one realizes that in giving his Word, God gives himself.[6]

Man in Contradiction to His Origin and Being

As shown above, man's origin, his essential being, and his destiny are grounded in the Word, the electing will, and the love of God. But this is not the whole truth about man. In reality, his entire existence is a blatant contradiction to all of this. To the very core of his being, he has become a creature of corruption.

He does not cease to be who he is as a responsible being before God; but in himself and in all of his relationships, he is an utterly perverted being. In his stubborn desire for freedom from every restriction and every claim upon him, especially the responsibility to answer God's Word, he has become, in Brunner's words, "Man in Revolt." [7] Modern man, in particular, has manifested an obsession for autonomy and therefore a disposition of isolated self-love.

In the biblical revelation, this contradiction is described as sin, which has brought about a cleavage in all that is human. To deal with this problem theologically in all of its moods and variations is one of the most critical tasks which confront the church in any age. Brunner adopts here (as indeed in the whole of dogmatics) the principle that a *Christian* doctrine must begin with the incarnate Word of God. This, he believes, frees him from bondage to the Old Testament narrative concerning the origin of sin and the fall, yet without surrendering any truth to be gained from it. Two considerations brought him to this conclusion. In the first place, he could see no evidence that the biblical view of sin, in either the Old or the New Testament, was significantly influenced by the narrative in the third chapter of Genesis. And in the second place, it appeared to him that many of the intellectual and theological difficulties involved in this problem were brought about by what he regarded as a mistaken attempt to relate it to that narrative.[8]

In his insistence upon the Christocentric basis of the doctrine of the fall, Brunner believes that he is strengthening rather than weakening that doctrine. The reality of the fall is in fact an important aspect of his theology. He sees it as an essential element in an understanding of sin, which in turn is the sole presupposition of the gospel of redemption. Apart from the fact of a fallen humanity, there could be no need for a Redeemer, and the message of the New Testament would be irrelevant. He insists, therefore, that his interpretation of sin and the fall is a departure not from biblical thought but rather from an ill-based ecclesiastical doctrine which dates back to Augustine.[9]

For Brunner, there is no simple, unambiguous definition of sin. He speaks of it as "the one great negative mystery of our existence."[10] And the question of the solidarity of the whole human race in sin is conceded to be the most difficult aspect of that mystery. Brunner is convinced that light is thrown upon this enigma only as one takes seriously his origin in the Word of God. Here, the individual man is always submerged in the whole human race, and the whole human race is always submerged in the individual man. From the creation, mankind is a unity in solidarity. Moreover, the solidarity of all men in sin is as much a reality as is the solidarity of all men in the creation.

Just as important, the Creator-Word of God is inseparable from the Redeemer-Word of God. And it is only in the unity of the Creator-Word and the Redeemer-Word that we begin to understand the unity of all men, including the reality of a unity in sin. The New Testament, according to Brunner, simply assumes the unity of humanity in sin (just as it assumes a unity of redeemed humanity in Christ); but it does not attempt to explain how this came about. The how, the where, and the when of both the creation and the fall lie outside the pale of human knowledge.[11]

A closely related problem has to do with the nature of sin. Sin is not merely something in man which is corrupt; it is rather the perversion of his very nature itself, in its entirety. In this light, man's being as a sinner is not contingent upon wrong decisions at a given moment. These momentary decisions leading to definite acts of disobedience, critical though they be, are only a reflection of the perverted tendency of our nature. In this connection, however, Brunner emphatically denies that sin is identical with human nature as such. He believes that nothing could be further from biblical thought than this.

Again, for Brunner, sin is never a quality, nor a substance, nor even a state. It is always an act, for the sinner always has his being as a person. The being of person and total act are inseparable. The New Testament knows sin only as a disobedient act of turning away from God. This apostasy, moreover, is continual and involves the whole of one's existence. In all that one is and does, he reflects his attitude toward God.[12]

Man in Conflict under the Law

If he lived in accordance with his origin in the Word of God, the truly responsive man would be in unhindered communion with his Creator. And this in turn would entail a loving relationship to his fellow-creatures. But with the one exception, Jesus Christ, all men have lived in opposition to their origin. In this situation, the will of God and the divine law of nature become grievously burdensome. As sinner, man cannot know the law as a means of love given for the enrichment of human life. He sees it only as a statutory demand, a bond by which God holds the rebellious creature in his hands and renders him inescapably accountable.

So to understand the law, according to Brunner, is to misunderstand it. Such a legalistic misunderstanding of the law of God cannot but inhibit "personal correlation," for it always interposes *something*, if only an abstract rule, between oneself and his God. The law of God, rightly interpreted, is nothing other than the twofold love commandment as set forth in Matthew 22:37–39 and further delineated in the thirteenth chapter of 1 Corinthians.[13]

In his origin, man's being is to live in the love of God and experience the joy of his Creator. But as fallen creature, he exists under the wrath of God, whom he can never escape. Just as the true being of man is an existence in the love of God, where alone is personal unity, so his being under the wrath of God is the dissolution of all personal unity, and therefore is an existence unto death. The sinner experiences the divine wrath as both a subjective and an objective reality. In this context, the law is apprehended as a curse.

It is at this point that Brunner finds the traditional ecclesiastical doctrine of man most unsatisfactory. According to that view, what is said about the original creation and the fall is focused upon one subject, "Adam," whereas what is said about the actual sinful state of man is focused upon another subject, one's own self. The result of this dichotomy in the understanding of the human situation is a distorted view of the actual conflict in human nature. One may therefore disregard the effect of the fall upon human nature; or he may overemphasize it to the point of degrading human nature.[14]

Man still exists by nature in the Word of God and therefore is responsible to the Word of God. Every aspect of his human existence suggests at once both the glory of his unique origin and the tragic perversion of his nature. In this situation, he has a perverted view not only of God and of the law of God, but also of his own essential nature, which means that he is in rebellion, not only against God, but also against his own essential being and destiny. He is in conflict between the truth of his origin and the falsity of his actual existence, both of which are in some form and to some degree always a reality.

The inevitable result of this tragic conflict, Brunner contends, is fear and anxiety, which have their ultimate ground in death. Man is thereby robbed of any genuine peace of mind and is left with an insatiable and inexplicable longing of soul. These fundamental and disruptive phenomena are also accompanied by others, such as doubt, despair, and bad conscience, from the nagging reality of which only a return to one's being in the primal Word of God can bring release.[15]

MAN IN SOCIETY

As creature, man stands first before his God. This primal fact of human existence gives direction and coherence to Brunner's entire anthropology. But man also has his being in the context of responsible relationship with other human beings. The task now, therefore, is to explore the meaning of this further dimension of his existence. Brunner sets forth his ideas on this subject in three of his major works: *The Divine Imperative, Justice and the Social Order*, and *The Christian Doctrine of Creation and Redemption.*

He begins with a general statement of the relation between natural morality and the Christian ethic, both of which revolve around the fundamental human question: "What ought I to do?" Brunner now proceeds to explore the implications of this question in the light of "the divine command" and of "the orders" within which Christian ethical life is to be sought and achieved.[16]

The subtitle of the German edition of *The Divine Imperative*, his major work on this subject, designates it "An Outline of a Protestant Theological Ethic." Thereby (and in contrast to Roman Catholic practice), he deliberately seeks to avoid removing the element of decision-making in personal responsibility. In the course of research for this study, he became aware, so he professes, that no work on ethics since the time of the Reformation had found its center in the evangelical faith.[17] This finding convinced him of the need for such a study and for the necessity of thinking through the ethical aspects of the concrete problems which arise within particular spheres of life.

The Problem of the Good in Natural Morality and Religion

Brunner observes that modern man tends to be relativistic, if not skeptical, as to the possibility of determining the good. Yet he contends that the problem of ethics is already present with the rise of human consciousness. Moreover, he sees all human action as in some measure a reflection of decision and of controlling principles as to what is right and good. Every decision is made in the light of some dominant purpose or norm or commandment. Brunner believes, therefore, that the ethical question belongs intrinsically to human existence. It is both theoretical and practical in nature. And while it is possible to neglect the theoretical aspect of it, the practical aspect cannot be avoided.[18]

Again, Brunner elaborates certain principles of existence which free the spirit of man from the actuality of nature and therewith supply human life with the character of a permanent order. He speaks of them as "stages" which mark the journey inward from undifferentiated immediacy with nature to the point of full self-determination. Through the power of reflection, the fact of immediacy with nature is broken and one moves on to self-determinative decision and thence to the mastery of nature for practical purposes. At this stage, however, even man-to-man relations remain on the natural plane, never rising above the level of mutual security and utility and such cooperation and exchange as are necessary for that purpose.

With the emergence of the moral consciousness and the spiritual principle of law, one is further freed from the bonds of culture, whereby he comes to a new appreciation of the present moment and its meaning for decision. At the same time, one's fellowman is also freed from that same bondage to culture, so that he too is seen as a person whose very being demands what Brunner describes as "unconditional respect and justice."

The journey inward by means of introspection eventually reaches its limits in the mystery of an inner law which one encounters in the form of a "thou shalt." Introspection now gives way to the question of religion and of divine revelation. The problem of ethics must therefore be examined in relation to, and in the light of, the religions of the world. This task, also, remains within the sphere of phenomenology.[19]

Brunner now turns his attention to the relation between morality and the phenomenon of religion. In every religion, he believes, there is at least a rudimentary idea of an all-encompassing law behind which stands an inexorable divine will. Even in the more primitive religions, there are awe-inspiring prohibitions which guard certain objects and spheres of life. And while the content of action controlled by such experience may not yet be described as ethical, it does indicate the fact of human deference to a mysterious power to which one is bound to submit or else stand in jeopardy.[20]

Brunner professes to see a deep underlying mutual influence between religion and the moral consciousness. Morality appears to attain its deepest profundity in the religious sphere and its clearest perception in the rational consciousness. Where morality does lose its connection with religion, it becomes increasingly bound to culture and its basis becomes secular. Likewise, where religion abandons the numinous (or nonrational, ritualistic element), it usually tends toward either a speculative, mystical pantheism or a moralistic, rational deism.[21] In the former event, it becomes ascetic in character, and in the latter, it becomes almost identifiable with culture.

At this point, Brunner examines attempts at the rationalization of the phenomenon of the moral in philosophical ethics. Here, there are only two great competing systems. On the one hand is the naturalistic system of ethics which is motivated by the desire for happiness and which in all of its varied forms undertakes to explain the moral life on the basis of natural facts and the phenomena of experience. It is thus inevitably utilitarian in content and outlook. To observe such laws as are thereby put forth is more a mark of cleverness than of goodness. This ethic (generally known as Epicureanism) is at once individualistic, egoistic, and eudaemonistic [22] in character. On the other hand is the idealistic ethic of "duty for duty's sake." Here, the principle of the good is sought, not in one's own natural impulses, but in that law which confronts one with the radical sense of "ought." The good is identical with obedience to the law. As a rational philosophical ethic, this system is characterized by immanence [23] and legalism.

Other forms of ethical theory have arisen between the extremes of the two systems described above. They have sought, without success, to solve the problems already posed by those two points of view. Brunner brings to an end his survey of philosophical ethics with the conclusion that each has its elements of strength and of weakness and that no one of them achieves a real synthesis—indeed that no kind of "synthetic ethics" can overcome the problems involved.[24]

The philosophical ethic of reason arose out of a felt need to undergird ethical thought with stability and clarity. But it has itself proliferated into a number of irreconcilable systems, none of which can solve the problem of the good.[25] Brunner is convinced that this problem can never be solved within the context of immanental ethics founded upon reason. The question arises, therefore, as to whether the ethical problem can be solved by religion—not, however, some rationalized, immanentist form of religion, but a religion of revelation in an "I-Thou" confrontation. What he has in mind here is a confrontation in which divine truth is not determined by man, but is rather received by him, and is himself thereby ordered.

Turning to a consideration of revelation, which can be received only in faith and ventured upon only as a confession, Brunner asks whether here is not found the answer to the question of the good. More specifically, he asks whether the ethical question does not find its answer given in full in the Christian revelation, and only there. Convinced that this is the case, he is now finished with what he calls "the purely phenomenological line of enquiry." Faith brings its own answer to the ethical problem. It is "the Word of Sin and Grace." [26]

The Christian Understanding of the Problem of the Good

The Christian answer to the ethical problem is grounded in the biblical message and its witness to the divine self-revelation. The Old Testament message, focusing upon the goodness and holiness and lordship of the Creator-God and his will for his creature, makes no distinction between the religious element and the ethical. The God-man relation is based on a covenant which demands utter fidelity. But while the thought of the Old Testament is "entirely theonomous and theocentric," it is also "entirely human and social." Unlike the religions of the world, there is here no separate sphere of the sacred, no dominant interest in the lone religious man, but a divine willing for community.[27]

Likewise, the New Testament combines the religious and the ethical. The norm of the good is in the activity of God alone. It finds expression in man only as he is willingly and harmoniously situated within that activity. Such is the understanding of faith; and this faith is the principle underlying ethics. Paul indeed asserts that "whatsoever is not of faith is sin" (Rom. 14:23). Again, in the New Testament it is made clear that ethics is a manner of life *in this world*. God does not take man out of the world, but comes to him in the world, as is decisively attested in the incarnation of Christ. At the climax of the incarnation is the supreme disclosure of love as agape, which is in turn the essence of the "new commandment" given by Jesus to his followers. Obedience to the new commandment is not only the meaning of the good, it is also identical with the will of God for his Kingdom.[28]

Thus, in both the theocratic idea in the Old Testament and in its fulfillment in the New Testament idea of the Kingdom of God, the good is manifest only in the sovereignty of God. When rightly understood, therefore, the church's dogma concerning the person and work of Christ secures "the Ethos of the New Testament against a pagan or rationalistic misinterpretation." And further, "the good" is delineated in the Christian message in such a way as to remove the difficulties surrounding that question in the context of the natural ethos.[29]

In the self-revelation of God, therefore, the Christian message provides the sole point of reference for an answer to the question of the good. This message stands in radical denial of man's self-derived understanding of his own nature, so much so that faith itself has its beginning only in the recognition of the error of the natural point of view. The whole life of faith, from its inception to the end of its earthly existence, is a continual conflict between the natural view of God and self and that which is supplied in the Christian message.[30]

In the light of its whole history, Brunner now expresses the firm conviction that natural ethics presents the specter of "a heap of ruins" and that "it is hopeless to attempt to construct a synthetic ethic." The Christian faith, unlike every attempt at a synthetic ethics is not based on any *principle* whatsoever, but upon the revealing and redeeming activity of God. And it is known only in faith.[31]

All forms of natural morality and ethics are seen as either eudaemonistic or legalistic in character, regardless of whether they are based upon religious or rational grounds. And even these two apparently divergent tendencies in such systems are ultimately one at the really decisive point, for both proceed on the assumption that man himself is the sole point of reference. Both are anthropocentric; both believe it to be within the capacity of man to attain and realize the good. Thus, the principles of self-seeking and self-reference dominate the whole of natural ethics.

Over against every form of the natural ethic, the Christian message proclaims that "all have sinned, and fall short of the glory of God" (Rom. 3:23), and, again, "none is good save one, even God" (Mark 10:18). But it also makes it clear that moral failure is already present in man's person before it manifests itself in the sphere of conduct. Therefore, even the assumption that one can simply achieve the good is itself evil; it matters not whether the basis of that assumption is Pharisaical, Stoical, or mystical in character. Above all, the Christian ethic is an unceasing struggle against every form of legalism, which, wherever it appears, makes genuine personal relation an impossibility.

Legalism, according to Brunner, knows only of a life composed of acts directed from a human center toward God, whereas the Christian message heralds a life which is received as a gift from the divine center which is God. Human life, even human righteousness, is dependent upon God alone. Where this truth is rightly perceived, Christian faith is no longer understood as a thing to be sought after and possessed. It is rather seen as a genuinely personal experience. Here, the law is not abolished; but it becomes a law without legalism, a law bound to love.[32]

For Brunner, the Christian ethic is not an ethical "system" based upon law and abstract principles. It does not simply tell us what we ought to do in terms of timeless propositions. Nor does it take from us the responsibility of making moral decisions. It does prepare us for the hearing of the divine command, in the light of which voluntary moral decisions may be made.[33]

The Divine Command

For Christian faith, the Word of God is the command of God, for in that Word, the man of faith is exposed to the divine will. The gift of grace is known to us in that call of God which is a summons both to himself and to his service. Prior to the experience of faith is the invitation, which is also a command, "Come!" And prior to every act of faith is the command "Believe!" The experience of believing is itself the receptive attitude of implicit trust and obedience.

The distinction and the relation between the *law* of God and the divine *command* are to be understood in the light of these truths. Every man may perceive the law of God in the form of conscience, but only in faith may one hear the divine command in the Word of God. The law, severed from grace, can be known beforehand; but apart from faith, it remains the law. Even the Old Testament commandments themselves remain in the category of law, until through faith they become the one divine command of love. But this divine command must be received afresh through the voice of the Spirit in every situation, for that command is the language of the Spirit who indwells the man of faith. Brunner sees the aim and purpose of his extensive work on ethics as an attempt to clarify that which can be known beforehand (the law) as over against the language of the Spirit (the Word of grace).[34]

In that division of his work in which Brunner deals with "The Divine Command," he departs from his usual procedure and begins each section with a proposition descriptive of its content. The first set of propositions has to do with the positioning of the basis and the norm of the good solely in the will of God. That will can be known only through the divine self-revelation in God's own Word. And as already indicated above, in the context of faith God's Word is understood as his command. But in this context, again, the command of God is received primarily as a gift—but also as a demand.

Of ourselves, Brunner believes, we cannot know the good, for it is not intrinsic to human nature. It is discerned through faith, however, where God manifests his own nature in the creation of the good, the giving of life, and the bestowal of self-giving love. Paradoxically, it is through his divine self-giving that he apprehends man as the servant of his will. Only in this context of his own utter self-giving may we begin to understand the meaning of the "new commandment" as the all-comprehensive command of love. And only here may we begin to discern that the good is in fact what God wills, that it can never be something done on a mere "principle" of love and thus attributable to the moral dignity of man. Again, the divine command is always concrete. It can never be discerned nor formulated in abstract, general terms. Hence, one cannot say beforehand what God commands. To undertake to do so would simply demonstrate a legalist frame of reference.

In himself, God is only one; and in itself, his action is only one. But in the historical revelation, he has given himself to be known in the twofold character of the Creator and the Redeemer. As Creator he is the source and ground of existence, and as Redeemer he is the end, the goal, of all existence—the one pointing to the past, the other to the future. In him are the beginning and the end. But we ourselves are situated in the present moment, that is, on the boundary between the past and the future and with no control over either. This is the perspective from which we may begin to understand the ethical significance of the present moment, where we have our existence. Here, at the center of time, where God reveals himself as Creator and Redeemer, is our "ethical moment of time." And here alone, under the aspect of the reconciliation achieved by Jesus Christ, may we understand what creation and redemption mean. That which takes place here, between the fall and the resurrection, is what Brunner did not hesitate to refer to as an "interim ethics."

The command of God as Creator is directed toward the preservation of the world. Here, everything is accorded its own appointed place and order of dignity. As it comes good from the Creator's hand, the world is expressive of the divine will. But in Jesus Christ we are given to know that this same world is no longer as it came from the Creator's hand. It has a tragic, sinful and broken existence which no longer reflects the divine will. In that situation, the will of God can be discerned only in the light of the original creation and of God's purpose of perfecting that creation. The will of the Creator now shows itself as the will of the Redeemer and at the same time poses a challenge to any passive acceptance of the world as it is. The command of the Redeemer is no longer one of a mere sharing in the work of preservation, but is one of participating in the work of the "new creation."

For Brunner, however, the command of the Creator and that of the Redeemer are not really divided. Each has its own mode of expression, but both are based upon the same divine love and will. Moreover, the unity of the command of the Creator and that of the Redeemer is realized only in reference to actual situations. Only in the light of these situations does one come to an appreciation of the longsuffering, preserving will of the Creator as being at the same time the will of the Redeemer to grasp, break, and re-create.

God's will is revealed in Jesus Christ to be one and constant and expressive of unconditional love. This will to love is also inseparable from his will to lordship. Behind the divine command to love, therefore, is the love which is the very nature of God and which he freely bestows. In this light, the command to love must not be understood in a legalistic sense, for "love . . . is the fulfillment of the law" (Rom. 13:10). To love is first to allow oneself to be drawn into the love of God, to let him take possession and do his own work of love through oneself. Where this takes place, there is no exclusiveness in the direction taken by one's own love; to love God and to love man are now seen to be inseparable.

The purpose of God's love is unchanging, but the demands of its content vary in accordance with prevailing circumstances and conditions in each human situation. Love, therefore, does not presume to know the good beforehand. It is this very fact that prevents its becoming attached to ethical systems, thus robbing the individual person of his responsibility for decision in every situation. To remain in the Word of God is to be subject to that

Word as it is given anew in the Holy Spirit in every human situation, and thus to remain bound both to God and to one's actual neighbor. In this light, the individual commandments of the Decalogue and of the Sermon on the Mount are seen not as mere laws, but as God-given examples illustrative of his will and of the application of love in certain concrete situations.[35]

Brunner's first set of propositions relative to the divine command dealt with the question of whether conduct is based upon the will of God. His second set of propositions has to do with the question of whether conduct flows from a personal existence which is determined by God. The focus here is not upon the will of God, but upon the "new man" as re-created and claimed by God. Investigation at this point proceeds upon the underlying assumption that Christian ethics is in fact only a division of dogmatics, and further, that a doctrine of man is contained in and presupposed by every ethical system.

In philosophical ethics, whether naturalistic or idealistic, the corresponding anthropology is more or less latent and is always defined in abstract, universal terms. In the naturalistic type of ethics, man is regarded as simply one form of nature, whereas in the idealistic type, he is looked upon as essentially divine. In Christian anthropology, however, man is identical neither with nature nor with the divine. As creature, he is a finite, corporeal being; yet, he rises above the natural in his capacity for sharing in the knowledge of God and in the reality of his proper existence in the Word of God.

On the other hand, Christian anthropology alone is aware of the fundamental perversion in the being of man, resulting from his sin and guilt. Because man is person, all of his acts and relations are personal. And again, because he is person, his sense of responsibility is never at rest. Awareness of responsibility either intensifies the condemning conscience or leads one to an experience of the new birth in the act of faith. In the event of the new birth, the self which was estranged from God is henceforth reestablished in the primal Word, and the new man finds his existence in the obedience of faith in the Holy Spirit. This means, of course, that God himself is the only subject and source of all good.

In the light of the divine command, any consideration of the good from the point of view of Christian ethics must ultimately shift its focus from action to being. This necessity arises from the fact that, in the final analysis, it is the acting *person* who is either moral or immoral, good or evil. Acts are only a reflection of what one is as a person. Yet, the Christian ethic is always directed toward that which is at once both given and demanded; and as something demanded, it must be concerned with acts reflective of that love into which one is called. To find one's true being is to stand in the love of God; but so to stand is to be drawn into his love for man, and love is never static.

Brunner now turns to a consideration of human "virtues" in the light of that goodness which has its origin and actuality only in God. Goodness has already been identified with that radical love which is the object of the one divine command. And love has been shown to be the only truly personal form of existence. The very possibility of human loving rests solely in that divine love into which the Christian man has been drawn. Alongside such a life of love, there can be no human "virtues" in the classic sense of the term. Brunner maintains that the very idea of individual virtues, in the sense of personal qualities, is not only presumptuous but stands in actual opposition to the Christian understanding of goodness. And in any case, goodness, as life in love, has only a relational meaning with respect to the needs and demands of others. The notion of virtues may be applied to that aspect of being which we designate as character; but personhood can never be conceived of as a combination of qualities. The question of individual virtues, he concludes, belongs more to the realm of pedagogy than to that of ethics.

A personal existence determined by God requires, further, that serious attention be given to the fact and purpose of self-realization. Brunner understands personhood as involving self-determination in conformity with the divine purpose and in accordance with that destiny which was set before man from the beginning. God himself confirms the new man in Christ, and he places upon that man the responsibility of affirming himself and his own individuality in gratitude before his Creator and Redeemer. On the other hand, to be in Christ means the death of the self-centered Ego. This self-mortification, however, has nothing to do with asceticism, for false isolationism and lack of fellowship lie in evil and not in good. The life of faith is a being in community as a responsible member of "the body of Christ." [36]

As seen above, conduct may be described as good only if it has its basis in the will of God and if it issues from a personal existence determined by God. Brunner now puts forward a further set of propositions which limits the good to that conduct which takes the form of personal service to one's neighbor. The divine command would thus draw one out of himself and make him free for others. In this context, it becomes clear that there is in fact no service of God which does not at the same time take the form of service to man. And this service, which ministers to the whole man, must be learned afresh from God in every concrete situation. It is never service on the basis of general "principles," but always has its imperative in the commandment of love in actual concrete situations. And it is God himself who hallows the means whereby the demands of love are met.

Such is the meaning of the Christian calling. A particular person is called to service in a particular situation and at a particular time. Brunner looks upon the Christian calling as one of the most profound truths of human experience. In obedience to the divine command, a radically new understanding of human response sets one free from every abstract notion of "duties" conceived of beforehand. Here, of course, "calling" is used in that theological sense which is heavily burdened with eschatological tension and which at the same time assumes a daring audacity in its confrontation of the world. It is at once a call into the world and a call out of it—a call to be in the world, but not of it. In the New Testament, it always has reference to a sharing in the "heavenly inheritance."

In the Christian calling, the sphere of one's labor, both in nature and in history, is perceived to be by divine appointment. Only in that calling does one learn the meaning of "neighbor," and only here does one in fact receive his neighbor as a gift from God. The person whom God wills as one's neighbor is now seen to be the very person one encounters—in the particular set of circumstances in which he is found. The will of God is now seen to be the basis of *this* person's life, also. Moreover, in accepting this person, one is obliged also to accept the communal "orders" in which he is given. This is the point where a Christian ethic must begin.

Brunner holds, however, that a Christian ethic must also give consideration to the will of God as Redeemer, for he wills not only the preservation of the created order, but also its perfection. Obedience to the divine command therefore entails both affirmation of and resistance to the existing sinful order. At best, this natural order is transitional. Faith requires that the service of love not be limited to its utilitarian value, but that it be expended also (and primarily) in view of man's eternal destiny. Behind the existing sinful orders, Brunner sees a divine order in the light of which every service of love is to be performed. He holds, therefore, that when an existing order ceases to serve a useful purpose and actually becomes harmful, "it is ripe for destruction." [37]

Here, we come upon a particularly difficult point in Brunner's thought. In their *historical* form, especially, he looks upon all of the orders (both those which he designates "the created orders" and those which he distinguishes as the "sinful orders") as "revelations of human sinfulness and godlessness." But he moves on to declare that "even apart from their historical forms" these orders "are revelations of the imperfections of the created world." They are at once "indications of the will of God for community" and also instruments of tyranny for an evil "collective egoism." They are obviously necessary to communal life; yet they are always "in danger of becoming idols by being transformed into absolutes," and thus becoming destructive of life, even to the point of "alienating man from God." Brunner observes that it is in this light that we must understand the will of God as a call both "to adapt ourselves, to accept, but also to resist" the world.

Brunner holds that God's created orders are effective in the whole sphere of human and sub-human life, extending even to "the lilies of the field" and "the birds of the air." On the human level, they are in some measure accessible to the purely rational mind, from the most primitive to the most sophisticated. But the ultimate meaning of these orders may be perceived only in the Word of God, where in faith he is known as Creator and Redeemer. There are also other orders of widely varying kinds, which, though not "pure orders of creation," nevertheless undergird the whole of life and are necessary to it. They are used by the Creator in the preservation of the world; and so, in a fragmentary way, are expressive of his will.

In contradistinction to the demands of the moral law, obedience to these "other orders" falls within the category of legalism. It is, however, a legalism which even the Christian is enjoined to engage upon; yet in doing so, he is to understand both its meaning and its limitations. As a member of his community and nation, the Christian also, along with everyone else, bears responsibility for these orders, even where one's official duty within the orders causes "pain and perplexity to his conscience," and where obedience seems to entail cooperation with an alien element.

Brunner argues that these orders are conceived and preserved by means of reason, that they are an aspect of that reality which precedes faith. Therefore, they are not subject to "the logic of faith or of love." But because they are the very basis and framework of human life, one's first duty is to work within them. The present existing order, however imperfect and loveless, is meanwhile the only effective resistance to the ever-threatening forces of chaos. As the only actual order, it must be preserved until such time as it may be replaced with a better one—and without discontinuity. This priority of duty within the orders is advocated in full recognition that one's official duty may entail a harsh, impersonal, and apparently unloving relation to others. Where, for example, one acts in the capacity of "a judge, a policeman, a bank official, a schoolmaster," he may not bring to the responsibility of this situation that which the command of love might seem to require in a private man-to-man relation. And again, the requirements of one's office within the orders may oblige him to do for the sake of order that which apart from this capacity would be positively wrong. Brunner holds that the conscious burden of this difficult situation can add a dimension of depth to one's petition for the coming of the Kingdom of God and a new urgency to his resolve to bring the vitality of love to the rigid forms of the existing order.[38]

Thus far, Brunner has indicated three necessary criteria whereby human conduct may be adjudged good. It must have its basis and norm in the will of God; it must arise out of a personal existence determined by God; and it must issue in personal service to one's neighbor. He now puts forth a final set of propositions relative to the command of God which focuses upon the actual works of love. These works of love take place, if at all, in the external, concrete world, where one meets his neighbor. It is the fact of this neighbor which renders one's external activity ethical in character, rather than merely technical.

This neighbor is encountered in the natural, historical world with the means and ends which are contained within it. It is this existing, sinful world with its means and ends which God himself sanctifies and uses for his own purposes, and which he requires us to use. These are the means and ends which are placed at our disposal by nature, civilization, culture, and society. All human action, and especially ethical action, depends upon them and upon the exercise of free choice in the devising of further ends. But Brunner insists that we may expect the approval of God upon our actions only insofar as they conform to the divine end of love.

The scope of individual ethical action, Brunner believes, is at best seriously limited in a world where one must depend upon technical means to make effective that which is freely willed.

Only the will, therefore, is fully free and responsible, for individual ethical action is at the same time participation in a collective life. The difficulty here is that both the "technical means" and the "collective life" upon which ethical action depends are impersonal. Both are aspects of the external world which is under the domination of autonomous forces, which in turn would counter the entire purposes of love.[39]

Christian ethical action must take place in the existing civil order and in conformity with the creative and redemptive purpose of God. Brunner describes this action as threefold in character. In the first place, it consists of "simple cooperation" with others in the various spheres of civil and cultural life. Here, one's action as a Christian conforms materially with that of nonbelievers and is determined by the same norms of justice, equity, and humanity as is theirs. In this category, his action may be described as "official" in character. In the second place, Christian ethical action consists of a more critical level of cooperation with others as a citizen working toward the realization of a higher form of social, political, and economic righteousness. Such action will utilize the available means to this end and insofar as possible, seek to improve those instruments and make them more effective.

And in the third place, Christian ethical action assumes an "apostolic" character, in which one enters the sphere of civil action as an avowed Christian. He openly works to bring his faith to bear in the practical problems of civil life, making it clear in word and act that he is there as a Christian. He is convinced that the desired change in the structures of social life are dependent upon a transformation of the very basis upon which it rests. Whereas the first two categories of civil action are of only temporary value, this professedly Christian action is believed to be of enduring worth. Obviously, cooperation here is possible only between those who share a common faith and purpose.[40]

Finally, the divine command reaches beyond the mere doing or giving of "something" to another, for such action is at best ambiguous. What is required is the giving of *oneself* to others in love. In this way alone does action become truly personal. To love is to enter into unrestricted fellowship, and the spirit which desires this fellowship arises in the reality of communion with God in faith. This means that a prior inward turning to God is fundamental to any genuine turning to one's neighbor in love.[41]

These statements of principle form the basis of an evangelical understanding of right conduct. They are fundamental to the Christian ethic. From this point on, Brunner turns his attention to the task of thinking through the implications of these principles in relation to the concrete problems which arise in particular spheres of actual life. These spheres, he admits, are selective, yet they are seen as divine orders within which one acts under the divine command. For his purpose, Brunner applies the principles of the Christian ethic to the relationships which prevail in community life (including marriage), in the economic sphere, in the legal realm, in the various forms of cultural interest, and in the community of faith.

V. The Christian Doctrine of the Mediator

The work which first established Brunner as a major theologian was *The Mediator*, published in 1927. This book has remained one of the outstanding contributions of this century to the theme of Christology. In choosing the person and work of Christ as the subject of his first extended doctrinal monograph, Brunner was already indicating what was to remain central to his theology to the end of his life. By his own admission, the motivation for this work was twofold. It was in part a reaction to the prevailing Christology of modern liberal theology. But more importantly, it was the result of reflection in faith upon the meaning of the biblical message and an expression of the conviction that for the Christian, there is ultimately only one article of faith—namely, that Jesus Christ is Lord.[1]

In the whole of Christian theology, but especially in reference to Christology, Brunner finds it necessary to try to unravel the purely rational and historical accretions from that which is divinely revealed. More than any other, this subject confronts the rational mind with the offense of the gospel. Central to that offense is the idea that man as sinner needs a mediator, through whom alone reconciliation between himself and God can take place.[2] This unequivocal emphasis upon the necessity for a mediator is that which more than anything else sets the Christian faith apart from the religions and philosophies of mankind. More than that, to trust in the one mediator, Jesus Christ, is the very essence of that faith.[3] This point of view is forcefully affirmed in a key passage in the New Testament, which reads: "For there is one God, and there is one mediator between God and men, the man Christ Jesus" (1 Tim. 2:5, RSV).

In *The Mediator* Brunner followed the natural and logical order of the traditional treatments of this theme. This meant that he dealt first with the person, and then with the work of Christ. But by the time he approached this subject in his *Dogmatics* some twenty-two years later, he had become convinced that it was more biblical to adopt an "inductive" method and treat the work of Christ first. He believed that the thought of Paul and that of the earlier primitive Christian community (in contradistinction to the later Johannine Christology) were much more occupied with the work, the gift, and the achievement of Christ than with the mystery of his person. He points out that the very titles given to Jesus in the New Testament are generally verbal and not substantive—suggesting that he was contemplated first in his action and only then in his person. And even where the mystery of his person does become a point of special interest, it is expressed in terms which indicate his work as well as his identity. He is still thought of and referred to in the language of verbal nouns, such as revealer, reconciler, and redeemer. For Brunner, this is a clear indication that the Christology of the New Testament is determined by "saving history" *(Heilsgeschichte)* rather than by metaphysical speculation.[4] In keeping with this point of view, therefore, it seems only fitting that the following review of Brunner's thought focus first upon the work of Christ and then upon his person.

THE WORK OF CHRIST

The Revealing Work of Christ

In actual fact, it is impossible to separate the work and the person of Christ, except for purposes of discussion. The gospel itself consists in the indissoluble unity of his work and person.

As soon as we begin to speak seriously of the revealing work of Christ, we are already deeply committed to the reality of his identity as the eternal Son of God. And on the other hand, to know that "God was in Christ" is also to know him as "reconciling the world unto himself" (2 Cor. 5:19). It is precisely this action in the historical sphere that directs our attention toward the eternal being of God, while at the same time accentuating more sharply than is seen elsewhere the contrast between the temporal and the eternal.[5]

The God-Man, Jesus Christ, is called the Mediator because in him the eternal Word is present. By his very existence he imparts to us something of the mystery of God. Thus Jesus could say, "he that hath seen me hath seen the Father" (John 14:9). The duality of the divine-human nature assures us on the one hand of the eternity of the Word that is given and on the other hand of the fact that the eternal Word has in fact come to us. To speak of the existence of the God-Man, therefore, is to speak both of that which is revealed and also of the very act of revelation. Likewise, to speak of him as the Mediator is to see him as both revealer and reconciler. Only faith can know him as the Mediator. But where he is thus beheld in faith, there can be no room for metaphysical speculation.

In thus emphasizing the mediatorial aspect of the *person* of Christ, Brunner does not in any sense intend to weaken the meaning of his *work*. He simply wants to call attention to the fact that in his person, Christ is the revelation of God. The meaning of the incarnation and that of the atonement cannot be separated. They both mean that God comes to us. The whole existence of the God-Man is God's great gift to us. The whole is to be regarded from the point of view of his self-emptying, his humiliation. The supreme element in his work is the fact of God's own presence in it, and the purpose of it is his final self-revelation.

In this regard, Brunner argues that it is essential to see both the historical and the eternal aspects of God's act in the Mediator. The historical facts of Jesus are indeed "a moment," but only a moment, in the revelation of God. They must be seen against the background of the eternal will of God and of his movement toward us. Otherwise, one may profess only to a knowledge of "Christ after the flesh" (2 Cor. 5:16), which Paul finds to be inadequate for the new creature in Christ. To know Christ merely "after the flesh," that is, only in terms of the historical facts, as important as those facts are, is not to behold *Christ* "in the flesh." Above all, one must see that it is in truth the eternal *Word* which has appeared in the flesh.[6]

Brunner sees the work of Christ as "primarily and preeminently" that of revelation. For him, Jesus was summarizing his mediatorial role when he prayed on the eve of the crucifixion: "I made known unto them thy name, and will make it known" (John 17:26). The purpose of God to make known his eternal will and to complete his work of love is the end which was served by Christ in the whole of his transitory act of humiliation. At every moment of his existence and in every act and word, he served that end. In so doing, he was often conceived of and even addressed as a Jewish rabbi, and thus a teacher of the *Torah.* But he was no rabbi in the ordinary sense of that term. He did not pretend to interpret laws and traditions nor to expound great truths. He simply bore witness to the reality of the Kingdom of God. Instead of dealing with the subtleties of forgiveness as a general truth, for example, he proclaimed forgiveness as a fact—and that with great authority.

He was also spoken of as a prophet. But Jesus was far more than a prophet. He did not simply proclaim the coming of the Kingdom of God. He dared to announce that the Kingdom had in fact come, and that in his own person. With authority he asserted: "But if I by the Spirit of God cast out demons, then is the kingdom of God come upon you" (Matt. 12:28). His understanding of the Kingdom of God was eschatological. Its wholly other character and the fact that it was present in his person was the basis upon which he could presume to forgive sins. In fact, his whole message was his word and action as determined by his consciousness of divine Sonship. What he proclaimed was already present in himself, for in him the transcendent and the immanent were uniquely one.

But again, Brunner makes clear that it was not as teacher or proclaimer, nor even as a historical personality that Jesus was the Mediator. He was the Mediator in virtue of the very mystery of his existence as the God-Man. Yet his teaching, illuminated as it was by his own consciousness of divine Sonship, belonged to the mystery of his person. This is why, except for him who "has ears to hear," even the most explicit speech of Jesus conceals quite as much as it reveals of himself.[7]

The Reconciling Work of Christ

At the center of the Christian faith is the message and the mystery of the cross of Jesus Christ. This is at once the "scandal of Christianity" and also that which most clearly sets it apart from every other form of religion or speculative idealism. At the cross, and here alone, the last vestige of intellectual and moral pride is shattered, for above all else it reveals man's absolute need for reconciliation.

Brunner holds, however, that the biblical understanding of reconciliation has often been misunderstood even by those who sought genuinely and seriously to interpret the meaning of the cross of Christ. One outstanding theological deviation in this regard is an overly subjective view of the passion and death of Jesus. This view, which still exercises considerable influence, was especially prominent in the nineteenth century in the thought of Schleiermacher and Ritschl. Its roots, however, reach back through the Socinians of the Reformation era, to Abelard of the twelfth century. Essentially, this line of theology adopts a humanistic approach to the meaning of the cross and therefore interprets reconciliation as a merely subjective process. One simply beholds and is inwardly moved by the example of this crowning act of fidelity to God on the part of Jesus. What one gains in thus gazing at the cross is understood to be only a clearer insight into truth already possessed. But this failure to understand the objective reality of guilt on the one hand and the seriousness of an objective transaction involving a divine act on the other makes it impossible to understand what the New Testament means by reconciliation. At best, reconciliation in such humanistic terms is only the removal of religious error and the clarification and deepening of religious truth. This view arose in the first place as a reaction against the defects perceived in Anselm's "satisfaction" theory of the atonement of Christ. Especially objectionable to theologians of this type was an idea implicit in Anselm's view that there can be a change in the mind of God.[8]

For Brunner, there can be no substitute for an objective understanding of the atonement. God has in fact revealed himself (come to us) in Christ—not in the pagan sense of a theophany where he might be known directly, but in the discernible and unmistakable "form of a servant" who became "obedient even unto death, yea, the death of the cross" (Phil. 2:7–8). Nothing could be further removed from the idea of an apotheosis of any description. Nor could anything be more objective than was this divine self-emptying. Christ's assumption of that which belonged to sinful man was not complete short of dying the death of a condemned criminal. All of this was incomprehensible foolishness to the secular Greek mind in its natural attraction to the purely aesthetic. The Greek mind could readily see its *folly* but had little capacity for discerning the offense which was involved. For the Jewish mind steeped in ethical and religious passion, however, the offense was unbearable. It was utterly unacceptable on two counts. In the first place, the typical Jew could not accede to the idea that it was the Son of God who died; and in the second place, he utterly repudiated the notion that this death was essential to the salvation of the pious and righteous Jew. For both Greek and Jew, the difficulty lay in an inability to see the necessity for reconciliation, because there was no understanding of the meaning of guilt.[9]

In the light of all that has been said concerning the awesome holiness of God and the utter perversion of man, the meaning of forgiveness is staggering to contemplate. It can become a reality only through the free will and gracious action of God. And it can be known only as it is divinely revealed to us. The meaning of forgiveness cannot be seen apart from the reality of guilt, of divine wrath, and of divine love. All of these facts are revealed simultaneously in the one reconciling event of the cross of Christ. Thus, reconciliation must be known, if at all, in an objective sense, for it is God who reconciles the world unto himself.[10]

The full meaning of the fact of the Mediator in being and act is not perceived until by faith he is beheld in his atoning death. Apostolic witnesses of that divine denouement were understandably at a loss for means to express it. But as finite men must always do in the presence of transcendent mystery, they drew upon familiar analogies and found ways to state, however inadequately, in parabolic fashion the meaning of what they saw. Sometimes they adopted figures from the practice of law, such as penalty and satisfaction. At other times they employed the more graphic cultic terminology picturing sacrifice and the shedding of blood. All of these express something of the truth which is involved, but no one of them, nor indeed all of them together, can say it all. They all merge, however, into one overarching idea of substitutionary and complete expiation. And in this great fact, we have what Brunner calls "the divine objective basis of the Atonement." [11]

If their language sounds alien and outmoded to the ears of modern man, it is nevertheless the witness of the primitive Christian church. Brunner holds that we cannot abandon their language without at the same time cutting ourselves off from their decisive and essential witness. And in any case, as he sees it, if we adopt more familiar terms from some sphere of life in our own age, they would be alien to the gospel if they did not preserve the same intensely personal and existential meanings which found expression in the primitive Christian witness. Likewise, as the history of modern man since the Enlightenment shows all too clearly, the subtle temptation is always present in the adoption of more appealing language to become anthropocentric rather than theocentric in the effect of what we say. Only the cross, and language appropriate to the cross, can express the reality that both the holiness and the love of God are equally infinite. And only such language can impress upon us the incomprehensibility of God: that when he is most near he is also most distant; that when he shows himself in mercy his holiness seems most austere; that in the very gift of his grace is manifest his judgment; and that in the attraction of his personal being is also the absoluteness of his majesty. What God is in himself and in his "coming," and what we are seen to be in the light of the cross of Jesus Christ—this is what the early witnesses sought to express through the figures which they used.[12]

The biblical message of the cross tells us in unmistakable language that neither sin nor divine wrath is an illusion. But at the same time, it assures us that there is a corresponding reality of divine expiation. And it is precisely the latter which tells just how grave are the facts of sin and wrath. Revelation reaches its highest intensity in the atonement at the cross. Indeed, Brunner states that where revelation and atonement are rightly understood, they are inseparable. Only in the unity of the two do we begin to understand the meaning of the Mediator. In *himself*, he is the revelation and the atonement, for what he is and what he does are one. By his very nature, in being and in act, the God-Man bridges the gulf between God and man. The way of the Mediator in its entirety is the way of the cross. Brunner understands the atonement, therefore, as substitutionary in the fullest sense of that word. It is an event which is vitally related to history; but it is far more than history, and as such it is accessible in meaning only to the response of faith.[13]

The foregoing has sought to show that for Brunner, the atonement begins with an objective, divinely given fact, an actual event culminating in the cross. The appropriation of that reconciling event, however, is a subjective process, which is the aim of the atonement. The point at which the objective and the subjective aspects of the atonement meet is in the Word of divine justification, which indeed is not heard except in faith. And since the relation between God and man is genuinely personal, faith in that Word of justification is the central point of the biblical message.

In Christ, God "comes" to us in an objective work and Word; hence our peace does not rest in the unstable character of our own religious experience. Yet, through the witness of the Holy Spirit, that objective Word becomes in the highest degree subjective. In the person and work of the Mediator we stand before the unfathomable mystery of God. That mystery is only deepened in the paradoxical combination of the objective and subjective aspects of the atonement. It is the mystery of the Son that God comes to us in objective manner; likewise, it is the mystery of the Holy Spirit that this objective coming is inwardly appropriated by the repentant sinner. Into the depths of these mysteries, Brunner holds that we cannot, nor should we seek to penetrate.[14]

The Dominical Work of Christ

Thus far, Brunner has focused attention upon those aspects of the work of Christ which center in the incarnation and the atonement. In both instances, the divine reality was seen as mercifully veiled in the form of the Mediator, for sinful man could not behold directly the majesty and glory of God except as wrath. But the revelation with which the Christian faith is concerned has to do with the whole movement of God—a movement which comes full circle only as a movement "from God to God." Behind that movement, moreover, is the sovereign will of God not only to restore the divine order of creation, but also to bring it to completion under his lordship. Therefore, the story does not end with the figure of the crucified one. Beyond that lowest curve in the descent of God lies the witness of Easter and the church of the resurrection: "we beheld his glory" (John 1:14).

The message of Easter emphatically declares that the whole

creation shares in his coming, that he is Lord over both life and death. This message is addressed wholly to faith, and it can be received only in faith. It is of such character that it may not be a mere object of reportage; only in faith may witness be borne to it. Only faith knows its meaning, for the Easter event stands uniquely alone. Brunner sees this event as the perspective from which alone the entire gospel is validated.[15] And beyond the Easter event, which marks the return of the risen Lord, is the ascension, the exaltation wherewith the goal of the whole movement of revelation is reached. Meanwhile, he exercises that hidden sovereignty which is known to faith; but the day is promised wherein he will "stand forth in His majesty" and we shall see him, the king in his glory.[16]

THE PERSON OF CHRIST

What may be said of the person of Christ has already been anticipated in part. In his person, he is the Word of God incarnate, a Word which is given in the form of an event, a Word which man does not possess except by faith and as a gift. This is the absolutely unique event which the Fourth Gospel introduced with the arresting words, "And the Word became flesh, and dwelt among us (and we beheld his glory, glory as of the only begotten from the Father), full of grace and truth" (John 1: 14). In this brief passage is summed up the whole of the Christian message. This Word in the flesh is the personal Word of Grace in which we have our true origin and destiny, for as John informs us, "as many as received him, to them gave he the right to become children of God" (John 1:12).[17]

For Brunner, the Word of God is utterly transcendent. Coming unknown, unsought, and unbidden from beyond the frame of our finite existence, it cannot first be judged or appraised, it can only be believed and trusted. Its authority rests solely in the evidence that it comes from God and has not arisen out of the rational processes of the mind nor out of the evolution of the human spirit. Whereas every prophetic word must point to a reality beyond itself (and for that very reason is only a provisional message), here is a Word which is also the embodiment of its message. It is the Word in which the personal God is present and gives himself to us in a personal form—that of the Mediator. For this very reason, Brunner believes, it can be at once either a rock of offense or an object of faith. On the one hand, it must be decisively rejected by every immanental form of self-assertion in the attempt to find essential continuity between God and man. It matters not whether that attempt is made on the basis of speculation, mysticism, or moralism. But on the other hand, where the Mediator is accepted in humble recognition of the reality of sin and guilt and the impossibility of healing from within all human resources, the attitude of trusting faith is born.[18]

The Deity of Christ

Trustful obedience to Jesus Christ, the Mediator, is the foundation of the Christian faith. His existence is presented to faith, however, not as a doctrine but as an act of God—indeed as the culminating act of the divine self-manifestation. When the proposition is advanced, therefore, that he is the divine Word incarnate, Brunner sees no room for speculation as to his identity, but only for decision regarding him. If through *himself* (and not merely through spoken words) he makes known the mind and will of God, he is in his own nature divine. Only as very God could he bring to us that mystery.[19]

Divine revelation does not belong to the realm of the historical personality of Jesus which, as the distinctly human element, might be known by any good historian. Rather, it belongs incognito to the realm of the divine being, the divine nature, and the divine authority. And again, as the Revealer, Jesus Christ is not to be seen as simply the bearer of an idea. He is in his own person the divine Word. The Revealer and that which is revealed are one. He himself, and not merely his message, is from eternity; rather, he himself in his coming *is* his message.[20]

Just here, however, we come upon an incomparable mystery,

for while the Revealer and that which is revealed are identical —one and the same God—there is nevertheless a distinction. One reveals, and one is revealed. Insofar as he reveals, he differs from that which is revealed. Brunner sees this as another way of saying that revelation is an actual occurrence. As the Revealer, God is the one who unveils to us that which is otherwise eternally hidden. As that which is revealed, he is the wholly other who inhabits eternity. It was the pondering of this divine enigma which first suggested the idea of the Trinity. In fact, Brunner holds that it was inevitable that the idea of divine revelation should eventually give rise to the doctrine of the Trinity. The truth which that doctrine seeks to express was already implicit the moment faith discerned that "God was in Christ" (2 Cor. 5:19).

This is in truth an impenetrable mystery (before which the New Testament remained silent), but it is not an illusion. And except for the fact that this very problem gave rise to heresies which in essence denied the unique character of the revelation, the refinement and formulation of trinitarian doctrine into ecclesiastical dogma might never have taken place. This means, therefore, that the dogma of the Trinity is a theological doctrine which exists only as a means of defense. It does not belong as such to the primitive scriptural proclamation. Both the doctrine of the Trinity and that of the two natures of Christ are "logical absurdities," but both seek to express what Brunner calls "the inconceivable miracle of revelation." Both attempt to deal with "the fundamental paradox that God became man." [21]

Brunner speaks of the doctrine of the Trinity as the completion of both the Christian understanding of revelation and the Christian doctrine of God. More than that, he believes that it enables us to pursue the significance of the two in union one with the other to the deeper understanding of both. God, as he is in himself, is not known to us, except in the personal God who "comes" to us (manifests himself) in the personal Word of revelation. In this light, the idea of "revelation" is as fundamental to a dynamic understanding of God as is that of "creation out of nothing." Both are finite modes of expressing the incomprehensible movement of the living God. Brunner holds that the most distinctive theme of scriptural thought from beginning to end is the threefold character of God, namely: that he is personal; that he is the Creator; and that he reveals himself in his personal Word. But with reference to the latter, Brunner insists again, that the genuinely personal Word can be only "the Word which has become Person." [22]

In biblical thought, revelation is always both form and content. This means that the very fact that God condescends to reveal himself is inseparable from the fact of his love. In revelation, what he communicates is not something, but himself. And this means that in himself, eternally, he is loving, that is, self-giving. Brunner sees this, and this alone, to be the significance of the Christian doctrine of the Trinity. In the context of the Trinity, the Word is the process of self-communication, yet that very Word exists eternally in God himself as the relation between the Revealer and that which is revealed. This is his very nature.

In himself and in his historical revelation, God is one who loves and gives himself; nevertheless, even in the act of revelation he remains the hidden God. While giving himself in love, he remains the sovereign Lord. Brunner understands God's love, therefore, to be expressive, not of his nature, but of his will. And in keeping with that point of view, faith is understood in the very personal context of being at once both gift (that is, divine presence) and intensely personal decision.[23]

The Incarnation of Christ

The biblical understanding of the self-revealing God sets him apart from every idea of deity arising from the side of man, whether of abstract thought, of mysticism, or of ethical idealism. For each of the latter forms of thought, God is conceived of in rigid terms of static truth; he is absolutely unmoved. The self-revealed God of biblical faith, however, is the God who, though unchanging, is nevertheless living, dynamic, and eternally loving—which is to say, he is in himself eternally in motion. In himself, he is love. The love of the Father for the Son, and that of the Son for the Father is eternal. In that same dynamic love, the world was created. And likewise, in that love God comes to the world for the purpose of redemption. That God *comes* is the ever-recurring theme of the Bible; but it is uniquely a biblical message.[24]

Brunner sees, however, that the coming of God may be understood only in the light of the reality of the gulf which separates God and man because of sin. He finds that sin, and therefore separation, are taken seriously only in biblical thought. And only here is it seen that the gulf of separation can be bridged by God alone. The self-movement of God to that end is the whole point of the Christian revelation. At the same time, that movement points up the fact that God and his initiative are absolutely central to salvation. And above all, it makes unmistakably clear the fact of the absolute sovereignty and glory of God and his will to bring light and life to the whole creation.

As already indicated, the coming of God in revelation and his coming in atonement and redemption are inseparable. This means that the knowledge of God and communion with God are also inseparable. Taken together, these facts indicate the important truth that the gulf between God and man is personal rather than physical and that the bridging of that gulf may occur only in a personal manner. Hence, God has willed to come to us in the only personal guise which we could receive—that of lowly human existence. In that self-emptied form, God really comes to us, meets us where we are and in so doing unmasks us, even as he unveils to us something of his own nature and will. Only in this context does Brunner speak of Christian faith, which for him is simply the attitude of humble personal reception, in utter abandonment of every self-contrived "way" to God. This means that faith (in contradistinction to every form of "religion") belongs to that range of exclusively biblical ideas which are expressed in such terminology as personal God, creator God, Word of God, coming of God, and revelation. Such faith exists only where there is the reception of the God who has come to us, namely, the Mediator.[25]

The revelation of God in Christ, according to Brunner, confronts man for the first time with that which is at once absolutely unique and absolutely decisive. Although it comes to man as a temporal event, it is eternal; and for this reason, it is absolutely decisive. Uniqueness has no place in a consideration of the natural order; at the very best, it is here considered as nonessential. And even in history as such, it has only relative meaning. Only the eternal element breaking into history can be absolutely unique, for it is at once the fulfillment and the abrogation, the end of history. The Word which comprises revelation is that Word which speaks of the beginning before all history and of the end (in the sense of purpose) which lies beyond all history. It is this eternal Word which breaks into history and gives meaning to decision. But the very fact that this unique event has occurred means that all of history has become problematical, that it lies under both the possibility and the necessity of decision.

This breaking-in of the eternal as an event in history is the proper concern of faith. Faith knows that it is anchored to that which transcends history because it is centered in the Mediator and therefore in the eternal self-movement of God. In fact, faith begins at the very point where historical perception reaches its outer limit. It understands revelation in terms of that incomprehensible movement of the living God which is manifest in the God-Man—Jesus, who is the Christ.[26]

Brunner now brings his argument to focus upon "the fact of the incarnation," which he describes as the "central truth of the Christian faith." The incarnation is seen as genuine, which means above all that the Son of God did in fact take upon himself our humanity in its fullness. But just at this crucial point, there was to arise a vigorous renewal of that fundamentally false assumption of the possibility of the self-ascent of man to God. It is propounded in the various forms of adoptionism which were to appear again and again in the history of Christianity. For Brunner, the essence of the Christian faith is retained or lost at this very point: that is, whether redemption is to be understood in terms of a descending self-movement on the part of God, and initiated by him, or of an ascending movement initiated and achieved from the side of man. No aspect of the Christian faith requires more clarity of insight and unfailing conviction than that which is involved at this point.[27]

What does it mean that the Son of God, the divine Logos, assumed human nature? How may we ascribe to him full and genuine humanity without losing the reality of the mystery of his being? This was the problem with which the patristic theologians of the fourth and fifth centuries wrestled. And it has proven to be one of the most difficult to hold in clear perspective. Brunner holds that it was just this human *nature* which he assumed. Behind human nature, even in our own case, and incomparably more so in his, is the mystery of personality. One *has* human nature; but he *is* a person. What Christ assumed was human nature, not human personality. This means that what he assumed was the genuine possibility of temptation and sin, but not that personality which is already corrupted by original sin. This, of course, points up the truth that sin is always a personal act, and never a fact of nature. The author of the Book of Hebrews states this truth in unforgettable language when he asserts that Jesus is not one who "cannot be touched with the feeling of our infirmities; but one that hath been in all points tempted like as we are, yet without sin" (Heb. 4:15). The mystery of human personality is sin, but the mystery of the personality of Christ is divine authority.[28]

Brunner speaks of the incarnation as "the great miracle" of Christianity and is emphatic in his assertion that "it is absolutely objective." Yet, he believes that it is the *fact* of the incarnation and not the *how* of it that is the proper concern of faith. He believes that the deeper meaning of the incarnation has been done a disservice by the traditional emphasis upon the virgin birth of Jesus. He believes that this emphasis has drawn attention away from the amazing fact of it in what has amounted to a rational attempt to explain in some measure the how of it. Apart from two brief passages (Matt. 1:18–25, and Luke 1:31–35), he finds that the New Testament shows no interest in this question. Brunner professes, however, that he has no particular interest in attacking the doctrine as such. He says: "We are . . . absolutely certain of the miracle of the divine fact." And for him, that fact presents us with two realities. One is that "the Son of God assumed the whole of humanity"; the other is that this "divine miracle does not permit us to offer detailed explanations" of it. Brunner sees the traditional emphasis upon the virgin birth as another expression of that docetic tendency which has always attended Christological thought. For his part, Brunner prefers to "stand amazed" in the presence of this miracle, without attempting to explain it.[29]

The Significance of the God-Man

The Christian faith insists equally upon the full deity and the full humanity of Christ. Brunner understands this to mean that the really decisive element in its message is that the eternal Word in fact became flesh. It is this which sets it apart from every thoroughgoing form of either transcendentalism or immanentalism. This is a self-revelation in that paradoxical form in which the glory of God is concealed in the very act of revealing. This is the mystery of the divine revelation. It is this concealed form of the revelation, however, which leaves room for genuine decision in faith. Direct and complete disclosure of himself by God would have meant one or the other of two things: either that he had undergone a metamorphosis after the fashion of a pagan miracle or that he had in truth unveiled to sinful man the fullness of his glory and majesty. The former would have been unworthy of him, while the latter would have exposed man immediately to the awesome and shattering power of judgment.[30]

But while this concealed form of the revelation makes room for faith, it is also open to misunderstanding. The substance of the Gospels may be seen as ordinary biography and therefore as historical in aim and character. In this case, they become mere reports of what happened on a human level, and when and where. From this point of view, the value of the Gospels is limited to historical interest and is subject to the degree of accuracy in reportage. Such a use of the Gospels, however, could only distort their true meaning and purpose and render them of little value for faith. On the other hand, there is always the danger that the humanity of Jesus shall be lost sight of altogether, in which case the Johannine Gospel would necessarily appear as docetic in character.

Aware of the problems involved for faith in these matters, the patristic theologians formulated the doctrine of the two natures: namely, that Jesus Christ is at once true God and true man. This formula, which was originally only a statement of faith concerning the unity of the divine and the human in Christ, was destined eventually to be transformed into a metaphysical theory, known in subsequent theology as the *communicatio idiomatum* ("the communication of properties"). Brunner sees this theory as an inordinate design to explain the mystery of the God-Man. It was essentially the view that the two natures, the divine and the human, were blended in one historical being. The doctrine of the two natures was thereby made the object of technical discussion and explanation in the same manner as any physical phenomenon. And this in turn meant an attempt to intellectualize faith.[31]

The divine person who meets us in the historical figure of the God-Man is visible only to the eyes of faith. Where he unveils himself, he is no longer seen as an historical personality, but as the eternal Son of God. The revelation itself is the mystery of this person, a mystery which is not removed but only intensified even where it is perceived as such by faith. And for Brunner, this means that there must be no attempt to explain the Messianic consciousness of Jesus.

God chose to meet us and to reveal himself within an actual human life on the plane of history—that is, in the person of Jesus. The question arises, therefore, as to how we shall regard the historical figure of the God-Man. Brunner insists that while the visible history of the life of Jesus is essential to the event of revelation, it is not to be understood as composing that event. The decisive element in that event is the eternal Word. And that Word is neither an idea nor a truth, but a personal reality. The New Testament itself showed little interest in many details which would have been essential to an historian's biography of the man Jesus. But its total witness is to the end that men may recognize in this man the Christ.[32]

VI. The Christian Doctrine of the Church

As an ordained minister, Brunner was a practicing churchman in the Swiss Reformed tradition. But for more than three decades, he played an influential role in ecclesiastical affairs in a worldwide ecumenical setting. During the thirties, he was deeply involved in the discussions which led to the formation of the World Council of Churches in 1948. And when the reality of this new organization directed renewed attention to the nature of the church, he was among the first to give it serious attention.

Brunner's formal contributions to the theology of the church are not as voluminous as are those in some other areas of doctrinal concern. Yet, they are important—and, one must add, are not always understood. Allusions to the church are frequent throughout his writings; but his principal contributions to this subject are *The Divine Imperative; Die Kirchen, die Gruppenbewegung und die Kirche Jesu Christi (The Church and the Oxford Group)*; [1] *The Misunderstanding of the Church;* and *The Christian Doctrine of the Church, Faith, and the Consummation.*

Almost thirty years before Brunner dealt with this subject in his *Dogmatics*, he was already speaking of the nature of the church as "the decisive question for theology." Even then he was calling attention to the significance of one's view of the church for a right understanding of faith and conduct. He was also distinguishing between the community of faith and fellowship on the one hand and those historical institutions which are commonly called churches on the other. The inadequate view of the church as expressed in certain classical definitions of it impressed upon him the necessity of wrestling with its meaning as both divine and human.[2]

AN HISTORICAL TRANSFORMATION

Universal concern with the nature of the church came at the opportune moment in Brunner's development of his *Dogmatics*. Just as he reached the point of dealing with this matter in his system, it was at the forefront of general theological interest. His preparatory volume on this subject *(The Misunderstanding of the Church)* took shape as a conscious participation in that debate.[3] And while he was conscious of the ambiguity in the title of this work, he chose it in the belief that it enabled him to come directly to deal with a fundamental flaw in the understanding of the church. It was his conviction that during the course of Christian history, the New Testament understanding of the church had undergone a radical transformation. Instead of being seen as a communion of persons, for which the New Testament uses the word *ecclēsia,* it had come to be conceived of as a church in the institutional sense. Brunner's principal thesis in this work, therefore, is that the identification of the ecclesia with the church *as institution* (in any form whatsoever) can rest only upon a misunderstanding.[4]

Brunner defines the alteration which took place as both structural and theological. The problem involved here is shown in sharpest relief in a comparison between the ecclesia as portrayed in the Pauline writings and the view of the Roman Catholic church as defined in the Codex of Canon Law of 1917. The change which transpired in the intervening time is interpreted as having taken place by minor, almost imperceptible, steps. From the papal point of view, this process represents a gradual unfolding of essential elements and characteristics which were already latent in the New Testament ecclesia. But from the Protestant point of view, each step in the process marks a further degree of alienation from the original and is seen therefore as an actual deformation of it. Each step is here regarded as bearing an adverse effect upon both form and content in the understanding of the church.[5]

Brunner now sets himself the task of examining some of those steps by which this transformation came about. He finds the first and principal point of departure from the original New Testament understanding of the ecclesia in the revised view of the Lord's Supper, whereby it came to be interpreted in a sacramental sense. Instead of being an act of faith and fellowship and an expression of common obedience and hope, it was now understood as an authentic means of salvation and was bound to an unwarranted assertion of formal and legal authority. Just as the fellowship meal had been the counterpart of the primitive ecclesia, providing visible unity in faith and hope and love, so now the idea of the sacrament was the counterpart of the church as institution and was the jealously guarded means of salvation.

This fundamental shift in the understanding of the Lord's Supper was accompanied by an equally basic sociological change in the structural conception of the ecclesia. Instead of being a genuine brotherhood rooted in fellowship with Christ, this body now came to be looked upon as a sacred institution with a holy priesthood through whom the sacraments were administered to the larger community of laymen. And as recipients of these means of salvation, the laymen bore an undefined relationship to the church. In contrast to the holy priests who stood as mediators at the altar and administered holy things, the laymen were regarded as profane and as representatives of the profane sphere of the everyday world.

The sacramental understanding of salvation was of necessity accompanied by the development of a sacerdotal system entailing a fundamental change in the understanding of structure and order in the body of believers. In the primitive Christian community, order was under the control of the Holy Spirit who distributed special gifts and ministry responsibilities. The exercise of gifts was functional in meaning and character and all of these appear to have been necessary and of equal worth for the body. There was no clear suggestion of rank or power among the members. Obedience was rendered only to the Lord himself. But now with the intrusion of a sacramental and sacerdotal outlook, there was also the emergence of the priestly bishop, who by his presence and through the administration of the sacraments functioned again and again to constitute the church. The sacraments were now seen to supersede the Word, and the original spiritual organism of the ecclesia gave way to legal organization. In short, the ecclesia became the institutional church. It was but a short step now to the idea of a monarchical episcopacy.[6]

Another very significant step in the transition from ecclesia to the institutional Roman Catholic church was the combining of the episcopal office and tradition. In the original ecclesia, tradition (known as *paradosis* in the New Testament) was understood to be the free transmission of that which had been received from Jesus himself. But with the establishment of the episcopal office and the investing of that office with regulative powers, the bishop now became the guarantor of tradition. In due course, the Holy Spirit's operation came to be regarded as bound up with that office, with the logical conclusion that the church is thereby preserved from error.

Thus fortified against the possibility of error, the church came to be looked upon as the repository of true doctrine. Its theological propositions were defined and set forth as binding tenets of faith, undergirded by ecclesiastical law. To deviate at any point from what was here prescribed was to be pronounced a heretic; and since the time of the Roman emperor Theodosius II (A.D. 401–450), heresy was punishable by the state. The meaning of this development was that free and spontaneous witness to Christ under the direct and compulsive action of the Holy Spirit was now replaced by a theology in conceptual form. The understanding of the gift of the Holy Spirit had now become materialized and his operation was conceived of as being at the disposal of men as the holders of episcopal office. This formulation of an ecclesiastical theology, and especially the official canonization of parts of it as dogma, played an important role in the establishment of the church as an institution.[7]

A further step in the transformation from ecclesia to established and holy institution has been associated with the changing status of this body in the world. With the decree of Constantine, which both legalized and adopted Christianity as the religion of the Empire, the Christian community emerged from the condition of a persecuted sect to that of a popular state church. And a few decades later, it achieved a compulsory inclusiveness as broad as the Roman Empire. But with this change of status, it underwent a radical and far-reaching modification in character as well. In the ensuing centuries, it became the rival of the state for status and authority.[8]

Even though he sees the widest deviation from the primitive ecclesia in the structural development of the Roman Catholic church, Brunner insists that it is also apparent in all the "churches," Protestant as well as Catholic. There have in fact been certain formidable and recurring forces in the history of Christianity which have pressed for a restoration of the primitive ecclesia, chief among which must be reckoned the work of the great reformers of the sixteenth century. But even the mainline Reformation churches retained a decidedly institutional character; and no organized Christian body is free from it.[9]

Brunner's conviction that the ecclesia had undergone radical transformation in the process of becoming an institutional church was forcefully argued in *The Misunderstanding of the Church*. Many of his readers and critics, therefore, were so taken up with this aspect of his thought that they apparently failed to notice, or at least to take seriously, that it was augmented by a further word of considerable importance to him.

Before he was finished, he sought to make clear that although he was insisting upon nonidentity, there are nevertheless elements of the ecclesia in all of the "churches." And further, he did not hesitate to speak of the institutional church as "shell" and "vessel" in which the ecclesia had been preserved. He even spoke of the churches in their most conspicuous form of alienation as potential instruments for the growth and renewal of the ecclesia.[10]

This more positive side of his argument is set out again, and perhaps a little more clearly, in the third volume of the *Dogmatics.* Here, he points out that within these historical churches, in spite of all deviations, the Word of Christ has been preserved and transmitted. And here, Jesus Christ has been believed in and confessed as Lord, which in itself gives evidence of the presence and activity of the Holy Spirit. It is in this sense that Brunner can speak of these historical institutions as "instrument and shell" of the ecclesia. He even suggests that apart from its "stern hierarchical structure," which is to say its institutional character, there have been times when these treasures could not have been preserved. This was especially true in the face of Islamic and Mongol invasions during the Middle Ages; and in perhaps a more relative degree, it has been true also in times of great migrations of people. This positive, preserving role has been played by all of the churches and sects of Christendom, each making its own contribution, however limited and imperfect it may have been.[11]

PERSPECTIVES ON THE REALITY OF THE CHURCH

What, then, is Brunner's view of the true nature of the church and its reality in the world? Perhaps the first thing which ought to be said is that this subject is yet another area of theology in which the significance of his idea of "personal encounter" is brought into sharp focus. He sees the ecclesia of the New Testament as "nothing other than a fellowship of persons" sharing in Christ and the Holy Spirit. This is its unique and

God-given nature. As the body of Christ, it is neither organization nor institution, but persons who are members one of another under the headship of its living Lord. Only in the presence of Christ dwelling within it through his Word and his Spirit does the ecclesia have its being. For this very reason, truth and fellowship are here experienced as inseparable—indeed, Brunner sees them in this context as "one and the same thing." And further, it is a visible fellowship which binds men not only to Christ, but also to one another. It is that new humanity which is described in the New Testament as the life of reconciliation.[12]

Brunner finds that there have been three classical definitions which have attempted to express the reality of the church. Each views the church from a different perspective, and each expresses something essential concerning the church's ground and nature, but no one of them is complete in itself. The first defines the church as the *coetus electorum* (the company of the elect) and ascribes to it a transcendent ground in the loving and electing will of God. Here the church is seen in sharpest contrast to any notion of a sociological institution. The second definition describes the church as the *corpus Christi* (the body of Christ) and sees its ground in the *corporate* fellowship of believers. Here it is clear that the church is not to be conceived of in Platonic terms as a merely spiritual reality. Neither is it only a tenet to be believed. It is rather a reality to be experienced. The third classical definition identifies the church as the *sanctorum communio* (the communion of saints) and grounds it in the faith of the *individual* members. Here, the church is seen as the community of the saints who have been individually called and added to the fellowship of believers.

Defined as the "company of the elect," the transcendent aspect of the ground of the church is preserved. But when this definition is permitted to stand alone, it leads to what Brunner calls "an abstract spiritual intellectualism" which interprets the biblical idea of predestination in terms of rigidly fixed numbers. Defined as the "body of Christ," the "historical-objective" aspect of the ground of the church is preserved. But when this definition stands alone, it leads to what Brunner calls "a sacramental hierarchism," as has been amply demonstrated in Christian history. And finally, where the church is defined as the "communion of saints," the "spiritual-subjective" aspect of its ground is preserved. But when this definition stands alone, it leads to "an emotional and pietistic individualism." Brunner holds, therefore, that it is only in unity that these three definitions can express the reality of the church as ecclesia.[13]

The foregoing definitions, together with their grounding, point to the spiritual and theological aspect of the ecclesia, which is apparent only to faith. But since the time of Constantine and Theodosius, a sharp disparity has been observed between this essential aspect of its being and its empirical reality. Augustine was already aware of this problem in the early fifth century, and undertook a rational explanation of it in his distinction between the visible and the invisible church. This distinction was again adopted in the sixteenth century by Zwingli and Calvin, who proposed to reform the visible church (that institution which is known to history) in accordance with their understanding of the ecclesia of the New Testament. They saw the visible church as an institution which existed for the purpose of proclaiming the gospel and of preserving pure doctrine. Calvin could thus speak of it as an external support of faith.[14]

Brunner regards this double concept of the church as a "desperate expedient" which has served more to confuse than to clarify the issue.[15] For him, there is only one ecclesia. The one entity is spiritual and invisible (and therefore discernible only to faith), and at the same time it is corporeal and visible (and therefore discernible to everyone). He sees the social form of this one entity as a necessary consequence of faith, for its very life is expressed in such personal matters as communication, reconciliation, and agape. This means simply that its social character is determined by its faith in Christ and is an outgrowth of the operation of the Holy Spirit in an association of men. It is a spiritual brotherhood which is bound together, however, by the working of the Spirit and not by any structural law of an institutional character. Any laws and institutions which may have become associated with it belong in no sense to its essence.[16]

Yet another problem of interpretation (which Brunner finds to have been especially pronounced in recent New Testament studies) also dates back at least to Calvin. This is the notion that the term *ecclēsia* is to be understood in the light of the Septuagint rendering of the Hebrew word *kahal* (which was understood as the "assembly" of the people of God) or in the light of the secular Greek meaning of the word *ecclēsia* (which refers to a popular "assembly"). Where this approach is taken, the New Testament term *ecclēsia* is understood as referring strictly to an *assembly* for purposes of worship. In both cases, however, the New Testament has added "an entirely new Christological content," whereby the emphasis is shifted from the assembly to the call (the *klēsis*) of God in Christ. And this transfer of attention, whereby the assembly (and with it, the cultic) plays only a subordinate role, brings into focus the ministry and mission of the ecclesia in the world.

Brunner believes that it is only in the light of this approach that the sociological character of the ecclesia may be seen in true correspondence with its genuinely theological nature. Through the secret operation of the Holy Spirit, the self-communication of God through his Word of grace issues in the self-communicating love of the brethren one for another as the very principle of life. Because this love is agape and not eros, the ecclesia is for Brunner "a sociological paradox." It is an intimate and visible fellowship of persons in close proximity; and at the same time, it is a new world-embracing humanity which knows no provincial limitations. Because its very basis is the call (the *klēsis*) of God, it is ecumenical in character. Here, there is one head and one body, which is a way of saying that the ecclesia can be understood only in and through Christ. Its visible, social character is the concrete manifestation of a genuine brotherhood. But if it is not visible in that way which is proper to it as the called, then it can be visible only in an improper way as an institution. And finally, whatever else may be said of it, the ecclesia of the New Testament was a social reality which not only drew to itself both Jews and pagans, but also left its enemies in puzzlement and wonder.[17]

THE ECCLESIA IN THE NEW TESTAMENT

Brunner is aware that in speaking of the ecclesia of the New Testament, it is possible to present a one-sided picture by failing to take into account the evident human frailties which were manifest in such primitive Christian communities as those at Corinth, Philippi, and Colossae. Further, one may fail to allow that while there was a conscious unity based upon certain fundamental aspects of the Christian faith, there were also important differences in outlook among these communities. At the Jerusalem Conference (described in the fifteenth chapter of Acts) we are given a glimpse of two different conceptions of the church in conflict one with the other. On the one side was the "theocratic-authoritarian" view of the Jewish-Christian communities, which were thoroughly legalistic in outlook. And on the other hand, there was a representation of the more free and open attitude of the Gentile-Christian communities, which were in effect contending for independence regarding an important matter of conscience.[18]

Among the New Testament writers, Paul alone left to us anything like an explicitly developed doctrine of the church. And in his case, what is said about the church is closely interwoven with his thought concerning the work of Christ and the experience of faith. Through his Spirit and his Word, Christ the living and present Lord binds believers together in a common fellowship and creates faith as a shared reality. The ecclesia has its existence in the proclamation of the Word, the reception of the Spirit, and agape (which is the necessary fruit of the Spirit). Thus, Brunner can speak of the ecclesia as something which "happens" of necessity wherever the Word of Christ is received in trust and obedience. Ecclesia is here understood as a life in which the call (the *klēsis*) is shared.[19]

Again, in Pauline thought the witness of those who beheld the resurrected Lord is essential to the existence of faith and the ecclesia. Their primary witness is the essential norm of the Christ-tradition for all time. But apart from that witness, they bore no further authority for the Christian community, nor did they pass on such authority to any successors. Christ alone ruled as the head of the body. Such human leadership as prevailed in these early Pauline Christian communities appears to have been strictly functional and subject to the charismata of the Holy Spirit. Yet, as Brunner sees it, a non-Pauline conception of faith and the ecclesia was destined to prevail. Both were to undergo radical transformation as elements in a legalistic, sacramental system.[20]

CREEDAL "MARKS" OF THE CHURCH INTERPRETED

This analysis of the church in its essence and in its historical development leads Brunner to reaffirm the essential "marks" attributed to it by the so-called "Nicene" Creed.[21] In so doing, however, he also provides his own exposition of the content and meaning of these marks. Taking them in reverse order, he expounds the meaning of each in its turn. He begins with the concept "apostolic," which affirms the word of Paul that the church is "built upon the foundation of the apostles and prophets, Christ Jesus himself being the chief corner stone" (Eph. 2:20). Brunner sees this as asserting not only its foundation in personal commitment to Christ, but also the important fact of its beginning in immediate proximity to the historical revelatory event. That is to say, its beginning is bound up with the account of eyewitnesses of the revelation in Christ. Like faith, the church is thus created (called into being) through the eternal Word and is an instrument of the Spirit. And further, to designate the church as "apostolic" is to affirm that its norm is the original ecclesia.[22]

Brunner now turns to the creedal affirmation that the church is "catholic." He understands this term in the teleological and normative sense, that in the purpose of God man was created with the God-given destiny of belonging to Christ. Hence, he was destined for the ecclesia: life in the ecclesia is the true human life. This carries the unequivocal missionary proposition that in the purpose of God the ecclesia is intended for the world. Catholicity is bound up with the most earnest missionary endeavor.[23]

The church is further declared to be "holy." In taking over this term from the patristic creed, however, Brunner is aware of a problem which must be clarified. He knows that those who formulated the creed thought of the church in the institutional sense, and therefore as an "it." He is also convinced that Paul refrains from using the word *holy* except with reference to persons. Brunner makes it clear that he uses it only in the Pauline sense in which the Corinthian church, for example, could be addressed as *klētois hagiois*, "called saints" (1 Cor. 1:2), or in the sense in which its task is conceived of as that of becoming *hagia kai amomos*, "holy and blameless" (Eph. 5:27). Here, participation in the holy is in no sense a participation in "things" understood as sacraments administered by an institution. It is rather a fellowship of persons in the call of Christ. In this context, "holy ecclesia" can mean only that life of faith which is grounded in and sanctified by the Word and act of God in Jesus Christ. It is made a reality by the Holy Spirit who alone sheds abroad in the hearts of the believers the love of God for his children. And this means above all else, the presence and lordship of Christ.[24]

The church is also declared by the ancient Fathers to be "one." Brunner also believes in the essential unity of the ecclesia; but his contention that it is not identical with the institutional churches is of vital significance here. He believes that in the institutional sense the difference between one church and a multiplicity of churches is of only relative importance. The particular form of a church is of little concern in comparison with the service it may render in common with the brotherhood of Christians resulting from faith in Christ. Where this insight is fully appreciated, the particular form of each church may be regarded as a special means for the accomplishment of the common task of Christ. In this light, the very multiplicity of institutions may be regarded as a positive value, each being seen as a different means, but all serving one end. For Brunner, therefore, the existence of a multiplicity of church bodies is not in itself the lamentable aspect of the current ecumenical scene. Rather, it is the failure to discern that the ecclesia is a spiritual brotherhood and not an institution.[25]

VII. The Christian Doctrine of Faith

Aspects of the Christian understanding of faith are already at least implicit in all that has been developed in the preceding chapters. It is appropriate, however, that full attention now be turned to this subject immediately following discussion of the ecclesia. For Brunner, the ecclesia and the life of faith are inseparable. To speak of one is to speak of the other. The witness of the ecclesia in Word and life is seen as the presupposition of faith, while faith is spoken of as personal existence in fellowship. Men come to faith only through the ecclesia; yet it is just as true to say that men come to the ecclesia only through faith.[1]

The subject of faith, by its very nature, is treated in some measure in a number of Brunner's works spanning the entire range of his literary production. His first publication in 1914 on the symbolic element in religious knowledge took the form of an ideological quest with reference to problems of social ethics and in reaction to the prevailing ideas connected with the Religious Socialist Movement.[2] But by his own confession, he was already searching for what he called "a scientifically satisfying formulation" of his faith. His deepest concern was "with the more fundamental question about God."[3] This was followed in 1921 by a study of experience, knowledge and faith, in which he undertook to restore faith to its rightful place in theology, as the necessary supplement of experience and knowledge.[4] Liberal theology seemed to him to have left no room for the activity of the Spirit nor for the reality and meaning of faith.

With his emergence as a theologian of repute on the international scene in the late 1920s, Brunner found himself in the position of interpreter of the new theology. A series of lecture tours during the next several years in different national settings provided opportunity for him to elaborate the central aspects of Christian doctrine, including the meaning of faith. The substance of these lectures is found in *The Theology of Crisis* (1928), *God and Man* (1929), and *The Word and the World* (1931). Two further brief works of practical significance for the meaning of faith were published in 1935. These were: *Vom Werk des Heiligen Geistes* (On the Work of the Holy Spirit), and his "popular compendium of theology," *Unser Glaube* (*Our Faith*). In the first of these, Brunner demonstrates a keen sensitivity to the work of the Holy Spirit and the meaning of faith in the tridimensional time sequence of human existence—that is, in terms of the past, the present, and the future. This time-sequence idea was applied and further developed a score of years later in a series of lectures entitled, *Faith, Hope and Love.*[5] In the meantime, he published *Der Römerbrief* (*The Letter to the Romans*)[6] in 1938. In this work, he meditates on the theology of faith as set forth in the incomparable letter of the Apostle Paul to the Romans. And finally, Brunner's most extensive and thorough treatment of the Christian doctrine of faith and the new life in Christ appears in the third volume of his *Dogmatics.*[7]

A PRELIMINARY DESCRIPTION OF FAITH AND UNBELIEF

A distinctive feature of Christianity is its understanding of faith. As employed by the Apostle Paul, the term *faith* is descriptive of a right relationship between man and God. It is a way of life, a manner of existence, and not merely an affirmation of the truth of certain doctrines. Man does not simply subscribe to or reject either a particular content or a special form of consciousness. Rather, he "*exists* either in faith or in unbelief." [8] Upon this premise, Brunner now turns his attention to a preliminary statement of the meaning of both faith and unbelief, in the light of the biblical witness.

Christian faith may be understood only in relation to human existence. It begins in the knowledge that the very notion of autonomy is a delusion, that one is not his own master but is under the authority of another. It has its inception in an encounter with Christ which is at once a disclosure and a removal of the craving for autonomy. Where one remains undisturbed in "dreaming solitude" with his own thoughts, he is out of touch with reality. Brunner perceives that it is only where that solitude is disturbed and resisted that reality may actually begin. Impersonal nature cannot disturb that solitude, for nature as such may be included in and brought under the mastery of human thought. Only the "Thou," through genuine personal encounter, may really disturb one's solitude and call in question man's autonomy. But where the autonomy of man is thus broken by the claim of him who is divine person and living Lord, a new dependency arises. And this event is described in biblical parlance with the term *faith.*

In the New Testament, however, faith is not only a word about dependency. It is also, and primarily, a message concerning the character of God's claim to sovereignty. Along with that claim is the assurance that God is also for man. Faith is thus related both to a divine claim and to a divine assurance that life is now provided with a new and sure foundation. God's coming to man is now seen not simply in terms of the shattering of presumptuous creaturely autonomy, but also and preeminently in terms of the ennobling and completion of human dignity. And wherever in the assurance of God, man receives a new being, he cannot but know that it is at the same time a restoration of his original being—a being who was created to dwell at the side of God and in unity with humankind. Such is the meaning of faith.

But what is the meaning of unbelief? From the Christian perspective, unbelief can be nothing other than an assertion of the will to autonomy, and that on the pretext of devotion to objective truth. Objective truth, however, is always impersonal and as such confronts man with neither claim nor assurance. In his autonomy, the unbeliever spurns the Word of God where alone he may recover the truth of his being in true *human* integration. Unbelief is thus seen to be in radical conflict with faith—a conflict which is at once the deepest problem and the most crucial issue of human existence.[9]

Brunner is well aware of the sweeping implications of his assumption that genuine dependence upon God is bound to faith in Jesus Christ. He now turns briefly to answer certain objections which have been raised to that proposition. The first objection is based upon the claim that certain non-Christian religions have in them elements which are of the character of faith. Brunner has no disposition to deny any real relation to God in these religions; yet, he stoutly maintains that such relationship as may exist is not that of absolute obedience and trust in response to the divine claim and promise, as must be the case in genuine faith. In none of them is to be found a personal encounter with the Revealer as Lord.

A further objection to the exclusive claim of Christianity in this regard is raised in respect of the close tie between the faith of Israel and that of the primitive Christian community. But again, while acknowledging that in the Old Testament the idea of faith is understood as man's response to the divine claim and promise, Brunner maintains that there are important differences as compared with the meaning of faith in Christ. In the first place, there is as yet no clear indication in the Old Testament as to the relation between claim and promise. More importantly, these are here present only in the form of prophetic utterance, whereas in the New Testament they take the form of personal and historical encounter. And again, in the Old Testament there is no clear distinction between faith and personal piety, with the result that faith is not yet seen in radical distinction from self-sufficiency and self-confidence. At best, faith in the context of the Old Testament is only an imperfect form of that which is advocated in the New.

And in the third place, it may be objected that even the nonreligious man is not necessarily to be reckoned as living under the delusion of self-sufficiency. Even as an unbeliever, he cannot escape the moral law, the "categorical imperative," the binding sense of ought which sets in some measure a limit to his own will. Yet, Brunner maintains that while the moral law is in some sense a denial of man's complete independence, it is also the most dangerous form of self-deluding autonomy. For it lends itself to the notion that what is ethically good is identical with the authentic self—that is, with the innermost will of the self. And on this basis, one justifies and confirms the self as good at its very core. Under no circumstances, therefore, may morality as such be equated with the Christian understanding of faith. It is only in encounter with Christ that the nonbeliever is able to see himself as he actually is. Only here does he realize that for man the decisive choice of his existence and destiny is a matter of faith and unbelief. And here for the first time, he understands why this is true.[10]

FAITH ACCORDING TO THE BIBLICAL WITNESS

In biblical thought, and only there, the fundamental relationship between God and man is understood as "faith." Yet, even in the Scriptures there is a marked development in the idea of faith. In the Old Testament, it does not yet occupy the dominating position which it is later given in the apostolic witness of Paul and John, though it is already moving in that direction. Even here, it is seen in decisive relation to the whole of human existence. And as a thoroughly personal act, it is already seen as human response to the call of God. Brunner holds, however, that in the very nature of the case, faith could not reach maturity until the fullness of God's self-communication in the Christ event.

According to the New Testament, the term *faith* is descriptive of the proper relationship of man to God. It refers primarily to the lordship of Jesus Christ and affirms that God actually meets us in Christ's person and in the historical events of his life, death, and resurrection. This faith was born in the apostolic community through exposure to him, quite apart from any mediating message about him. It was first expressed in the form of acknowledgment of him as the divine Lord, a conviction which was immeasurably deepened by the events of the resurrection and Pentecost. The apostles now saw him as the Word and the Act of God and as the substance of the "good news" which they were to proclaim abroad. They felt themselves actually laid hold upon and overcome by a new spiritual power, an inner compulsion; and this they called *faith*.

The substance of the primitive Christian proclamation was especially developed by Paul, but it was based upon a common apostolic confession which antedated his own experience of faith. The object of faith was Jesus Christ himself, and not merely some doctrine about him. And because of its thoroughly personal nature, the apostles conceived of the experience of faith more in terms of a being apprehended, than of an apprehending of some particular body of content. For them, however, the experience of faith and its content were inseparable. It could find expression only in full obedience and trust, based upon genuine repentance in the sense of *metanoia* (a change of mind).

Only in faith, Brunner argues, does God's self-communication find completion, for only here is his glory and love mirrored back to him. Here, God's being for man has its counterpart in man's being for God. Only in this personal relation does faith reach its culmination in the certainty of the inner witness of the Spirit. Faith is a double act on the part of man in response to God's self-communication: it is at once self-surrender and acceptance of the God who comes to him. It is the response of one who acknowledges his own judgment and condemnation in the cross of Christ. And at the same time, it is humble and grateful acceptance of the divine restoration of one's original dignity, the glad and exalted response of one who has been called from death unto life.[11]

In the writings of the New Testament (especially in the writings of Paul) the revelation in Christ and faith are so inseparably bound together as to be given the same dignity. Faith is often spoken of as the one condition upon which the work of Christ may come to fulfillment.[12] Moreover, it can even be used in the absolute sense, where it matters not at all whether one uses the word *faith* or the word *Christ*. Brunner interprets the coming of Christ and the coming of faith as two different modes of speaking of the same event.[13] The one may not be realized apart from the other. Brunner holds, therefore, that a genuine understanding of the New Testament meaning of faith is "the principal task of theology."[14]

AN HISTORICAL MISUNDERSTANDING OF FAITH

As shown above, Brunner sees the ecclesia and the life of faith as inseparable. He holds, therefore, that what happens to one in the course of history cannot but have its effect upon the other. And this is what in fact did happen. As the ecclesia gradually took on the character of fixed institutional form, the primitive idea of faith also became hardened into rigid orthodoxy. Instead of being the free response of personal encounter, faith now became assent to authoritative formulations of doctrine. Brunner refers to this radically altered view as Credo-credo (Belief-belief) faith. Here, an unmistakable distinction is drawn between the objective truth of faith (regarded as Credo) and the subjective appropriation of faith (regarded as credo). Just as faith in the personal sense of trust, loyalty, security, and obedience was the true counterpart of the primitive ecclesia, so belief in prescribed doctrine now became the necessary counterpart of the church as institution. Henceforth, a Christian was regarded as one who believed what the church set forth in binding creedal form.[15]

This historical misunderstanding of the Word of faith is also significant for its effect upon the meaning and role of witness. Brunner sees that there are in fact several elements in the primitive meaning of witness, which all belong together. But he discerns a tendency to isolate these elements, with results which are detrimental if not actually misleading. In the first place, he believes that witness may take the form of *narrative*, incorporating the significant facts of the life, death, and resurrection of Jesus. Faith does indeed rest upon these facts as a sure foundation. Herein lies the historicity of the Christian faith, which distinguishes it from other religions and at the same time preserves it from docetism. Yet, the historical misunderstanding of faith has led all too often to the notion that it is first simply a matter of belief in facts, upon the basis of which one then believes in Jesus Christ as the Son of God. In this regard, Brunner believes that the Gospels are more concerned to present Jesus as the Christ than they are to fill in the "facts" about him. In other words, faith is not assent to the historian's account of the "facts" of Jesus, but rather it is response to the believing testimony to this Jesus by those who beheld him as the Christ.

In the second place, Brunner understands witness as taking the form of *explanation* as to the meaning of the facts of the life and death of Jesus in the light of the resurrection. And again it must be admitted that explanation is a genuine and necessary element in faithful witness. It is an essential aspect of doctrine whether it be simple or profound. Yet, Brunner believes that the doctrinal element in witness may be so isolated that it takes the form of a declaration which must be believed. This amounts to an abstract doctrine which simply asserts with authority that Jesus is the Son of God. Here, one is called upon to believe in a *doctrine*, which may not at all involve one in a personal encounter with Christ through the Holy Spirit.

In the third place, Brunner believes that witness may take the form of an *authoritative word* to nonbelievers on the part of those who have in truth encountered the living Lord. This element of witness is of course vital to the propagation of the faith. No words can be so convincing as are those which are spoken out of the fullness and the warmth of that love which is poured out in the hearts of believers. But where this happens, it cannot be comprehended in any doctrinal formulation. At best, doctrine can be only an objective *article* of faith, bearing all the finitude of human apprehension and grammar. And to insist upon the final authority of such doctrine, even though it emerges from the community of faith, is to claim for that community the primary adherence of faith. Indeed, it is to ascribe to that community the presumptuous role of essential mediation of that faith to Christ.

Finally, Brunner affirms that witness may take the form of a word spoken from within the believing community, to the believing community. Here, faith speaks to faith, ecclesia to ecclesia. Where it is true and vital, spoken in the power of the Spirit, it is a Word which actually creates ecclesia. Brunner contends, however, that all too often an overemphasis upon orthodoxy has led to an insistence that faith *begin* with an acceptance of the Bible as the infallible Word of God. This, he holds, is often given precedence over the matter of faith in Christ and the principle of justification by grace alone. He sees this order of concern and this emphasis as representative of a rationalistic faith in the Bible which corresponds to faith in dogma. In other words, the true object of faith (the living Lord) is thereby in a measure supplanted by the words which are borne in testimony to him.

Brunner holds that all of these elements must be held in conjunction if witness is to be a unique activity in the New Testament sense of the word. Witness is not to be identified wholly with any one of these elements, yet they all belong to witness. And all of these elements "find their unity in God's self-communication in Jesus, the Christ." [16]

THE WORK OF CHRIST THROUGH THE HOLY SPIRIT

In his exposition of the meaning of faith, Brunner touches again in his *Dogmatics* upon several of the key ideas in his theology. Among them are the emphases upon the multifaceted self-communication of God, the personal character of the divine-human encounter, human responsibility in the Word of God, the surrender of autonomy on the part of man, and the lordship of the Creator-Redeemer God in history. He seems especially sensitive to the reality of the many-sided work of Christ through the Holy Spirit in the man of faith. Several aspects of that work and its results are highlighted in his analysis of the experience of faith. These include not only matters related to the inner personal and transforming character of the Spirit's activity, but also its meaning for Christian existence in the world.

Experientially, the new life in Christ is an indivisible unity. Only for purposes of theological analysis may it be dealt with in terms of particular aspects of its multiform nature. For this purpose, however, it may be dissected and examined with reference both to the divine activity and to the human response and results. Brunner now turns his attention, therefore, to a treatment of such basic subjects as justification, regeneration, conversion, and sanctification.

Justification

Brunner speaks of the Pauline doctrine of justification as both "centre and climax" of the gospel. Indeed for him, justification is not in the first instance *doctrine* at all, but rather the assurance of a forgiving, reconciling Word addressed directly to the convicted sinner by a gracious God. In this experience, the self-communication of God meets its goal in that human response of faith which is divinely sought. The Word of justification and faith are so coordinated that Brunner can speak of the former as the "perfected form" of the latter.[17]

The nature and meaning of justification and its relation to faith are brought to a focus in Romans 3:21–31. Building upon his prior conclusion of the universality of sin, Paul here makes clear that in the same moment in which the depths of one's own sin is unveiled, so also is the self-bestowing love of God.[18]

Brunner begins at this point to expound the Pauline doctrine of justification. Like Paul, he finds two essential elements in the idea of justification, both of which center in the cross of Christ. In the first instance, judgment concerning one's own sin is spoken from the cross. Here, and here only, is one reduced to nothing in himself as he encounters God in the one truly righteous man who is crucified. But the sinful man who knows himself thus judged and who lets himself be identified with the cursed one dying on that cross hears yet another Word. This is a Word through which the condemned sinner is also identified with the righteous one who is acceptable to God. Justification, then, is that unique encounter in which sinful man hears in utter seriousness both the "No" and the "Yes" of God. But it is an encounter in which the "No" is completely submerged and absolved in the "Yes."

Justification means that God declares the sinner righteous; and thus once more this man finds his original, authentic being in the Word of the Creator. Not only does he hear that Word (Brunner calls it "the naked Word of God"), but he opens his heart to receive it and obediently repeats it, entrusting himself to it as an unqualified "venture of faith." This he does, not upon the authority of any dogma, but through the operation of the Holy Spirit whose free and direct witness to Christ gives rise to faith. Just here occurs that coincidence of objective divine self-communication and subjective human self-understanding which Brunner understands to be the very basis of dogmatics.[19]

Regeneration

The expression *justification* is a strictly Pauline figure taken from the context of jurisprudence. It carries the distinct connotation of an I-Thou relation in which the Word of God brings forth a new creation. For this reason, Brunner prefers it to other New Testament terminology and figures which are employed to describe the same experience.

Another figure which is also used in this connection is *re-*

generation, otherwise expressed as a new birth. When rightly understood as a figure and not a natural process, the term *regeneration* contributes to a richer understanding of the meaning of justifying faith. It suggests the *totality* of the new creation in the Word of God. It connotes the character of the new being in Christ as *life.* And it points up the reality and *effectiveness* of the Creator-Spirit of God in the new creation. That which was at odds is thereby reconciled, and that which was hopelessly reduced to chaos is thereby reintegrated. A new self-identity takes place, so that one may say with Paul, "it is no longer I that live, but Christ liveth in me: and that life which I now live in the flesh I live in faith" (Gal. 2:20). Assurance of that fact is wrought through the inner testimony of the Spirit who himself "beareth witness with our spirit, that we are children of God" (Rom. 8:16).

Regeneration consists in the death of the old man and the formation of Christ in the new man of faith, which means in effect the integration of personality at its very core. But Brunner sees it also as the agent of unification and wholeness on a broader plane, namely, in the creation of fellowship on the part of those who are thus renewed in the Word of God. The miserable solitude of sinful separation from one's fellowman is thereby overcome through incorporation in a new humanity. In finding personal wholeness, the regenerate man finds also the capacity for genuine fellowship in the body of Christ.[20]

Conversion

As already amply indicated, the divine-human encounter involves the reality of serious personal correspondence. This calls for faithful and continuous "correlation between divine revelation and human responsibility," which is to say that God's faithfulness and regal claim demand the human response of trust and obedience.[21] At this point, however, Brunner finds it necessary to come to grips with an apparent difficulty which Martin Buber has raised regarding the biblical understanding of faith. Buber contends that the apostolic theology of Paul and John is radically alien to that of the Old Testament (and even to that of the Synoptic Jesus) at this point. Indeed, he sees their thought as irreconcilable with *personalistic* faith on any grounds whatsoever. These apostles seem to him to be advocating a gnostic interpretation of the "fact" of Christ, a mere doctrine to be believed, with no room for response on the part of the human subject beyond that of intellectual assent.

Brunner points out that Buber's difficulty is not really that of a distinction between the faith of trusting obedience on the one hand and a mere belief in a "fact" on the other. In other words, it is not a question of the *structure* of faith as such, but rather that of a distinction between the substance of Jewish faith and that of Christian faith. For as Brunner observes, even in the Old Testament, faith is response to "God's action in historical events and in the prophetic Word." And this is precisely the meaning of faith in the New Testament—namely, *human response* to a divine event on the plane of history. Buber's objection to the apostolic understanding of faith is further weakened by the reminder that in Peter's famous confession at Caesarea Philippi (so central to the gospel tradition), he was not simply accepting a theology, but rather the person of the Messiah.

An answer to Buber's criticism is especially important for Christian faith in view of the biblical emphasis upon conversion. In both the Old and the New Testaments, the idea of conversion refers to a voluntary turning away from one's own chosen way to that of the revealed will of God. Brunner includes in his treatment of this term the biblical meaning of repentance as expressed in the Hebrew word *shub* and the Greek word *metanoia.* It represents a call to a change of heart, a change of mind; but more than that, it is a *total act* in the highest and fullest sense of responsible personhood.[22]

Brunner sees a positive dimension in the conversion experience, an act of obedience in which one not only acknowledges divine condemnation, but gives himself over to death. Identifying himself with the man on the cross, he confesses with Paul,

"I have been crucified with Christ" (Gal. 2:20). But this very dying with Christ is also accompanied by the poignant conviction: "Christ died for me." And so to confess is already of the very essence of faith. Moreover, this turning about, which is the meaning of *conversion* (or *repentance*) includes the act of putting on "the new man, that after God hath been created in righteousness and holiness of truth" (Eph. 4:24). The life thus reorientated is further attributed to all of those who "walk not after the flesh, but after the Spirit" (Rom. 8:4). Such is descriptive of the truth of our being as created by God.

Conversion marks the end of autonomy and the acknowledgment of one's Creator and Lord. In this experience, the Word of God becomes an inner Word in which the Holy Spirit renders the Christ event truth in a twofold sense: truth about one's own self and truth about God. And even the reception of the Holy Spirit is contingent upon the reality of obedience. Peter's charge at Pentecost was: "Repent ye . . . and ye shall receive the gift of the Holy Spirit" (Acts 2:38). As Brunner puts it, the Holy Spirit "happens when men hear and obey." And finally, conversion is also a new orientation to one's fellowman, a movement out of self and into the world in the interest of the Kingdom of God. It involves active participation in the winning of the world to Christ.[23]

Sanctification

Sanctification is yet another term descriptive of the work of the Holy Spirit in effecting the new life in Christ. As a work of the holy God, it is the act of setting apart for his own purpose that which otherwise stands in opposition to his will. Like each of the terms treated above, it refers to a different aspect of the same experience of faith. And like each of the others, it preserves the reality of "personal correlation" in the "divine-human encounter." Brunner sees it as at once a work of God and a response of man.

In biblical thought, sanctification always means a putting at God's disposal that which is alien to him. Yet it may be described in two different ways, depending upon the particular emphasis intended. It may be used in a broad general sense which includes the divine side of justification, regeneration, and conversion. From this point of view, it marks the *act* by which Christ through the Holy Spirit takes possession of the whole of one's existence, rendering him a *saint* in the New Testament meaning of that term. This is suggested, Brunner holds, in the way Paul addresses the Corinthian church. After describing various prevalent forms of scandalous human behavior, the apostle charges: "And such were some of you: but ye were washed, but ye were sanctified, but ye were justified in the name of the Lord Jesus Christ, and in the Spirit of our God" (1 Cor. 6:11). Henceforth, though one is still far from perfect, he is nevertheless the peculiar possession of the redeeming God.

There is also another point of view from which the term *sanctification* is used in the Scriptures. Here, the emphasis is not so much upon the act (in the sense of a specific and unique event) as upon a gradual growth *process*. This view of the matter is especially compatible with the New Testament understanding of the Living God as present and active in the world. The noncontingent eternal Lord of all being is seen to indwell and concern himself continually with the temporal sphere of relativity. He has his creature in his hands, so to speak, which means that we are not yet what we shall be, for as Jesus said: "My Father worketh even until now, and I work" (John 5:17).

These two meanings of the idea of sanctification are really not essentially different in effect, for both have to do with bringing to God's disposal that which is otherwise estranged from him. Taken together, however, they do indeed indicate a paradoxical tension in the character of the Spirit's activity in human life. The first declares that by God's justifying act one is already that which according to the second meaning he shall in fact become. And in this double sense, sanctification is a restoration of that which God originally created and pronounced good.[24]

As already indicated, sanctification also includes the positive response of man to the act of God. And if from the divine side it consists initially in the *justifying act* of God, from the human side it consists primarily in *conversion* from an existence in estrangement to a new life in Christ. In the bestowal of grace, God also lays upon us the summons to obedience, which points up the ethical side of sanctification. Thus Brunner finds that there is a divine and a human side to the one happening, a mutuality of grace and obedience.[25]

He sees two ways, however, in which the human side of sanctification is especially open to misunderstanding. On the one hand is a tendency toward legalistic moralism, which is unable to free itself from the regulation of binding rules. Such an attitude not only deprives a believer of his rightful liberty in Christ, but also robs him of genuine spontaneity of love in human relations. Immediacy with God through the Holy Spirit is thereby denied, for something (namely, the law) is allowed to remain in between. For the Christian, moralism indicates an overemphasis upon sanctification as a process contingent upon duty. But on the other hand is an equally serious misunderstanding which takes the form of quietism in its almost exclusive emphasis upon the gift of God.

Brunner contends that neither moralism nor quietism is a fair representation of the New Testament understanding of sanctification, for there grace and obedience are inseparable. In Christ, there is at once the supreme gift of grace and the unequivocal summons to discipleship. One is indeed called first of all to a new being in Christ; but the new being manifests itself continually in action which is also new and transforming. Sanctification, though never complete in this world, points nevertheless to that true humanity where one is rightly related both to God and to his fellows. Meanwhile, it presupposes watchfulness in prayer, and faith that Christ is conqueror over every otherwise insuperable hindrance to that end.[26]

COGNITIVE AND FUNCTIONAL ASPECTS OF FAITH

The theological foundation of Christian faith and knowledge was examined in the second chapter of this book. Attention was there given to the question of truth as the fundamental basis of both faith and knowledge. The question must now be raised as to whether faith *is* knowledge. For modern man, however, knowledge tends to be an epistemological concern which has already been conditioned for him by both Greek philosophy and modern science. He manifests a strong predilection for grounding all knowledge in nature, with the science of physics as its model. If this were a valid assumption it would mean, of course, that objectivity is as important as exactitude and that knowledge is simply the apprehension of the object as it is in itself, quite apart from any element of subjectivity.

Drawing upon findings in the areas of biology, sociology, psychology, and idealistic philosophy, Brunner now undertakes to demonstrate that naturalistic objective explanation cannot be the basis of all knowledge in general. It cannot account for such phenomena as human consciousness, human conscience, and human responsibility. Neither objective explanation nor subjective understanding can penetrate to the source of human responsibility. Nor can they provide release from the burden of human guilt. At best, they can do no more than lead one to the boundary beyond which only faith can reach. But just here at this boundary, faith is born and lays hold of that knowledge which can be apprehended only through the historical revelation in Jesus Christ. The meaning of responsibility and guilt both find an answer here, but only in a Word which comes from beyond one's own observation and analysis.

In this Word, Brunner discerns that the stark reality of responsibility and guilt is radical indeed. For here, one stands before the Crucified (the *innocent* one who died a criminal's death) and must assent to the poignant pangs of conscience with the confession: "He died for me." And beyond that affirmation in the Word is another which is yet more utterly a matter of faith. It is the assurance that whereas Christ rose from the dead and men "beheld his glory" as the Son of God, so also the man of faith shall be resurrected and stand revealed as a son of God.

In the light of this Word, Brunner asserts that the question as to whether faith is knowledge is crucial. It surely cannot be "objective" knowledge, he believes, for what one knows in faith is not an object, but absolute Subject. Nor can it be knowledge in the sense of rational understanding, for it arises at the very boundaries of understanding. Yet, faith is knowledge—and of a quite singular kind. It is knowledge of a reflexive nature in which one is given to know that he is a sinner. At the same moment, it is also an interior exchange in which one is assured that he has been appropriated in love as God's own possession. Such knowledge is not and cannot be mere cognition. The situation here is the same as with truth. If it is biblical to say that one does not have the truth yet may be *in* the truth, it is also biblical to say that one does not merely have knowledge but is in knowledge. And it is just this knowledge which is in the process of transforming one's very existence. Meanwhile, Brunner affirms that one must confess with Paul: "For we know in part . . . but when that which is perfect is come, that which is in part shall be done away. . . . For now we see in a mirror, darkly; but then face to face: now I know in part; but then shall I know fully even as also I was fully known" (1 Cor. 13:9–12).[27]

One further observation must now be made. Where there is not the possibility of objective knowledge, Brunner sees no possibility of rational certainty either. Rational certainty is the ideal of the autonomous solitary self. The certainty of faith, on the other hand, is the ideal of the theonomous self, for faith rests in the Word of God. In the words of the biblical writer, "faith is assurance of things hoped for, a conviction of things not seen" (Heb. 11:1). Faith, therefore must utterly reject every demand for proof as an expression of unbelief. Indeed, doubt can arise only in vacillation between reliance upon God and an untrusting demand for proof. Doubt arises where one no longer continues steadfast in the Word of God, which is to say, fails to remain in living encounter with God.

The certainty of faith, however, does not consist in passive repose, but in active and trusting obedience to the divine Word. It has its life in living encounter with God in a real world, where there is always the possibility of unbelief. Indeed, Brunner sees the life of faith as a continual returning from the actuality of unbelief. Faith must therefore be continually reborn in genuine repentance as one hears and responds to the Word of God. This Word is the home of faith, its only ground of certainty. There can in fact be no certainty of faith except as God gives it. Brunner finds the classic expression of both aspects of faith in Paul's description of his own experience: "I press on, if so be that I may lay hold on that for which also I was laid hold on by Christ Jesus" (Phil. 3:12). This means, of course, that faith is not yet sight. It must live meanwhile as an eschatological hope, which is to say, "the hope of glory," where every cause of doubt will be forever removed.[28]

The life of faith in the real world is one of tension and eschatological reserve. It bears the marks of impersonal existence in a fallen world, yet through anticipation and prayer it already shares in a Kingdom "not of this world." Faith finds dynamic expression in prayer, which is a kind of withdrawal from the world, an experience in which, from the side of man, transcendence appears under the guise of actual event. Brunner brings his discussion of the new life in Christ to a climax, therefore, with a brief examination of the theology of prayer.

The content and character of faith, Brunner believes, are put to the test in the actual practice of prayer. Nowhere else is the whole of one's theology so pointedly brought to account. And yet, the very notion that man may enter into meaningful communion with God is nothing short of scandalous to the thoroughgoing rationalist mind. For such a one, it appears as gross presumption that a mere man should invoke the unseen God and expect to be heard. This attitude can and does prevail only where God is conceived of in terms of abstract ineffability; and here, of course, the only reasonable stance is one of silent reverence. But we have not so learned the God of biblical revelation.

The God of whom Jesus taught, the God who comes to us, who gives his name to be known, is the God who ordains prayer. Prayer is response to the self-communicating God, the very essence and fulfillment of human destiny. It embodies the whole compass of theological understanding and concern far more perfectly than does doctrinal formulation, be it ever so refined. In true Christian prayer, the I-Thou relation of Creator and creature is expressed in genuine fellowship. Yet, there is here a reckoning in the light of what each participant brings to this encounter. God remains what he is, even while listening to and granting the requests of the man who thus prays. Jesus made it clear that the will of God is not done until prayer is both made and answered. Brunner holds therefore that it is only in man's disposition to engage in the full range of prayer that theological reflection takes seriously the meaning of faith.

He affirms, moreover, that God hears and answers every prayer which is genuinely uttered in the name of Jesus; yet the divine answer need not wholly conform to the intention of the one who prays. In every petition, he believes, there must be that reserve which Jesus himself demonstrated in Gethsemane when he prayed: "nevertheless not my will, but thine, be done" (Luke 22:42). Faith does not strive to change the will of God, but to find and conform to that will. And this it does in the knowledge that before prayer is supplication it must needs be adoration and praise and thanksgiving. The ultimate end of the prayer of faith is now seen to be the glory of God. And so to engage is to anticipate that dimension of eternal preoccupation for which in Brunner's view man was created.[29]

VIII. The Christian Doctrine of Eternal Hope

As already indicated, Brunner performs the task of dogmatics within the magnificent framework of the self-communication of God. That divine activity is presented first in the light of its eternal foundation and in regard to the nature and the will of God. Then follows an examination of its historical realization in terms of creation and redemption and in relation to the ecclesia and the new life in Christ. It remains now to look at the divine self-communication as consummation in eternity. This scheme indicates a conscious attempt on the part of Brunner to represent history and all theologizing under the aspect of eternity. The divine self-movement has not only its inception but also its purpose and fulfillment in eternity.

In approaching his discussion of eschatology, Brunner makes it clear that in reality he has already been concerned with this subject in everything that has thus far been said. For him, eschatology is not a mere appendix, either to Christian life or to Christian doctrine. It is written boldly across the whole of both life and faith. It is the working out of faith in its fullness by the God who comes to us in the actualities of history and moves that history toward his own goal. He may in fact be apprehended only in reference to the goal toward which he is working in the world. And so to speak is already to introduce the theme of eternal hope, for faith does not exist apart from hope.[1]

Brunner's principal contributions to the subject of eschatology were produced at a time when ecumenical interest in this area of theology was at its height. His basic thought on this subject was published in 1954 under the title *Eternal Hope.* This work was presented as a preliminary contribution to the theme of the World Council of Churches' general meeting which was convened later that same year. That theme was "Christ—the Hope of the World." The following year, he delivered the Earl Lectures at Pacific School of Religion in Berkeley, California, a series which was later published under the title, *Faith, Hope and Love.*[2] The second of these lectures deals with that time-dimension by which the Christian already lives in the future through hope. And finally, Brunner presents a distillation of his most mature thought on this subject in the third volume of his *Dogmatics,* which was published in 1960.

THE SIGNIFICANCE OF HOPE FOR HUMAN LIFE

Hope as the Coalescence of Time and Eternity

Hope is described by Brunner as "the presence of the future" and as the "mode of awaiting the future." [3] As such, it is essential to human life in both its intellectual and its spiritual dimensions. Only as humans do we really have a future and a destiny. *Hope,* therefore, is one of the primary words of the New Testament descriptive of the new being in Christ, a word which is fundamentally associated with faith and love.[4] Specifically *Christian* hope is firmly rooted in the objective content of biblical faith and is already implicit in that faith. It lives, however, through the experience of personal encounter in that present in which the Christian has his existence.[5]

The concern of biblical faith with history sets it apart from most religions of mankind. Oriental mystery religions have no interest in history because of history's transient character in contrast to the eternal. And the polytheistic nature-religions, with their view of the cyclical processes of nature and time in eternal recurrence, leave no room for history. History is possible only in relation to a purposeful goal toward which time is seen moving in linear fashion and under the control of an intelligent and reliable being. And further, history is possible only in terms of responsible personhood on the side of man. Brunner believes that these two essential elements, the historical and the personal, are taken with utter seriousness only in the Christian faith. And only in that faith does he find allowance being made for the reality of a coalescence of the temporal and the eternal, in accordance with which it could be affirmed: "And the Word became flesh" (John 1:14).[6]

More fundamental than the problem of history, however, is the meaning of time. This was long regarded as the special concern of philosophy; but eventually it was seen to be of vital significance for theology as well. Only in the very recent past has its importance for the message of the New Testament been generally appreciated. The question now arises as to whether there is a specifically *Christian* view of time, and if so, wherein it is unique.

Brunner holds that all men have in fact *experienced* time as linear, but that there are radical differences in the way they have *interpreted* this experience. Some men have understood their being in mythological terms as identical with nature and nature itself as bound by fate to a never-ending, ever-revolving process. According to this view, time is not only circular, but is of the essence of eternity. Nature, time, and man himself participate in the eternal. A second interpretation, which gradually emerged from the mythological view, arose among the philosophers of India and Greece. These men represented a shift of focus from the essence of nature to that of eternal truth, and they saw truth itself as unaffected by the temporal process. They approached the problem of time and transience from an ontological perspective, judging everything in terms of being and nonbeing. Linear time was understood as an unceasing movement out of the "not yet" into the "no longer"—which meant that for these men, time was constantly passing into nonbeing. True being, on the other hand, was regarded as timeless and as having no essential relation to the temporal process. Truth, likewise, was regarded as timeless; and so were the ideas by which truth was thought. Furthermore, the conscious subject who thought these timeless ideas was believed to participate in the eternal in the very process of thinking of the truth.[7]

Christian faith rejects both the cyclical view of nature-mythology and the abstract philosophical notion of timelessness. It sees time as linear, encompassing the temporal span from the creation of the world to its consummation—a view which it inherited from Judaism. But more importantly (and this, in Brunner's view, sets Christianity apart from every other system of thought and belief), it sees eternity itself revealed in one unique event in time. Both time and eternity, and their relation one to the other, are here understood only in the light of the Christ-event. Moreover, the entire range of being in time (in past, present, and future dimensions) is thereby given a new orientation in accordance with ultimate reality. Thus, Brunner can speak of the life of faith as eschatological in character and meaning.

Where time and eternity are thus fused in the experience of the believer, a radically new understanding of both is already apparent—and indeed is essential. Time is understood as created: like the physical world, it had its beginning. Likewise, it will have its end. It moves in a straight line from a beginning point toward a predetermined end or goal. In this manner, it becomes *historical* time. Beginning and end are held in suspension by the Lord of time, and in accordance with an eternal plan. But this is already to begin to speak of eternity.

God alone transcends the span of time in all its dimensions. In him, past and future are bound up in a divine present which is indivisible. Past and future (faith and hope) are thus given to us in a present which is known to us as love—God's love, his very being. In the light of the high-priestly prayer of Jesus, Brunner understands this love in terms of an eternal dialogue between the Father and the Son (John 17:24). It is this love which has been "shed abroad in our hearts through the Holy Spirit which was given unto us" (Rom. 5:5). And this love Brunner identifies with the *eschaton* (last things), that which will abide when all else has passed away.[8]

Hope and Unbelief

As already indicated, Christian hope arises out of an objective faith and in conjunction with a serious view of time and history. But it has not remained unchallenged in the face of the real world of experience. From different perspectives, it has been opposed by the reality of unbelief. Brunner takes note of two major categories of unbelief which have been manifested in modern times. One of these, he believes, was based on the erroneous presupposition of the objectivity of all knowledge. On this premise, men like Ludwig Feuerbach and Sigmund Freud regarded religion (including Christianity) as mere wish-projection and the belief in transcendence as an illusion. In their commitment to objectivity, they each adopted the stance of mere spectator and thus lost sight of the reality of personal responsibility before God.

A second, more subtle, category of unbelief was based on the secularization of the Christian hope. Arising on the very ground of traditional faith, yet deviating radically from it, certain substitute hopes were put forth with far-reaching influence. One of these was the widespread belief in the idea of progress. This notion was of rationalistic, bourgeois origin and was based upon what Rousseau called the "perfectibility of reason." It flourished especially in the nineteenth century and was impressively espoused from three different sides, namely: the idealistic philosophy of history, the evolutionism of Charles Darwin, and the advances in modern technology. The illusion of this false hope was effectively destroyed in the wake of two world wars, the rise of totalitarian states, and the development of nuclear bombs.

The most devastating form of secularized Christian hope is what Brunner refers to as the "Marxist eschatology." This phenomenon represents an aberration from the Hegelian philosophy of history. On the basis of a change in fundamental principles, Marx exchanged the absolute idealism of Hegel for an equally absolute materialism, whereby matter and not spirit was conceived of as the dynamic and controlling factor in history. Here, the idea of God is regarded as an illusion and the notion of a creation is rejected. The Marxist program, moreover, calls for the nationalization of all of the means of production and of the whole of life, including man himself. This means in effect the functionalization of man, and therefore his dehumanization.

Brunner is convinced, therefore, that apart from the certainty of Christian faith there is only hopelessness, for hope is grounded solely in the living God. Christian hope does not exist apart from the struggle of faith in the actualities of history; but it is struggle in the assurance that the decisive issue has been resolved in the death and resurrection of Jesus Christ. Hope is ultimately bound up with the conviction that man may indeed find the true end and fulfillment of his being in the Kingdom of God.[9]

HOPE AND THE KINGDOM OF GOD

Brunner understands the Kingdom of God as the final realization of the divine will. Its coming marks not only the consummation of humanity and of history, but also the very purpose and goal of the divine self-communication. Its content is nothing less than the absolute sovereignty and love of God, which together constitute the ultimate reality. This divine Kingdom is already present in the person of Jesus Christ; and in an imperfect degree it is present in the fellowship of those in whose hearts he reigns as Lord. The dynamic of this new reality is the presence and power of God as the Holy Spirit. For Brunner, life in the Spirit and eschatological existence are one and the same thing: it is above all life in love, in the sense of agape, in which the ecclesia is created. Only in this light may we understand the significance of the divine self-communication. God, who is agape, does not merely reveal himself; he also communicates something of his own nature to those who thus know him, so that they too are characterized by agape.

For this reason, and without identifying it any closer with the

Kingdom of God, Brunner can speak of the ecclesia as that new humanity who do in fact experience the presence of Jesus Christ in the Holy Spirit. Yet, like the Apostle Paul, he thinks of that experience as only the "first fruits of the Spirit" (Rom. 8:23). The ecclesia meanwhile must wait for the full harvest. It lives in paradoxical anticipation of that which is in some measure already experienced. What we await is the perfection and completion of that divine presence which we already know in part. The same thing is expressed somewhat differently by another New Testament author in the following manner: "Beloved, now are we children of God, and it is not yet made manifest what we shall be. We know that, if he shall be manifested, we shall be like him; for we shall see him even as he is" (1 John 3:2).[10]

The New Testament employs two different modes of expressing the eschatological hope, each of which points up a different aspect of the one reality. The first of these is the phrase, "the Kingdom of God," which seems to indicate the universal scope of God's purpose of redemption. The second is the expression, "eternal life," which seems to indicate more specifically the individual character of salvation. Brunner holds that when the two are seen together, they disclose the real contrast between the Christian hope on the one hand and both Jewish apocalypticism and Hellenistic gnosticism on the other. It is distinguished from Jewish apocalypticism in that it is professed to be a present reality. It is distinguished from Hellenistic gnosticism in that the knowledge it proclaims is declared meanwhile to be incomplete. Furthermore, the point of reference in each of the New Testament modes of expression is Jesus Christ, the Lord.[11]

Finally, Brunner sees the Kingdom of God as the meaning and goal of history. He believes that there have been two decisive moments in human history. One of these occurred with the birth of Greek humanism when man discovered himself as a reasoning being in contrast to nature. With that one event, the subject of history was at once discovered and distinguished from nature. Yet, by thus defining his essential being (his humanity) in terms of reason, man saw himself as also withdrawing from history and participating in the eternal Logos. Thus, while discovering the realm of history, Greek humanism at the same moment denied its essential importance for man who was believed to participate in the suprahistorical.

The other decisive moment in human history occurred among the people of Israel. Here, God himself came to be regarded as the true Subject of history. And here, likewise, man was ascribed a place of preeminence in relation to other beings and events. But whereas in Greek humanism the distinctively human endowment was seen as reason, in Jewish religious thought it was regarded as ethical and practical obedience to the will of God. In this context, history was understood as a struggle, indeed a drama, of divine sovereignty and human rebellion. That struggle reached its climax and its meaning was fully disclosed in the one Christ-event.

Brunner holds that in contrast to natural events, there is a relative sense in which historical events always have something of the character of the unique about them. But he sees the Christ-event as unique in the absolute sense. Faith in that event, therefore, is seen as true historical existence, for in Christ it perceives the very basis and meaning of history and the truth about humanity. But this means in the final analysis that the meaning of history must come from beyond history. It comes in Jesus Christ in whose person is manifest the reality and the meaning of the Kingdom of God. Christian faith holds that in his coming in humiliation he revealed both the purpose and the meaning of history. Christian hope holds that in his coming in glory he will consummate all things.[12]

HOPE AND THE MYSTERY OF DEATH

Man is different from other creatures, both in life and in death. Every attempt to find the meaning of his life within the range of earthly historical existence is utterly frustrated by the reality of death. And *human* death remains as an impenetrable mystery. The physical sciences (such as biology, physiology and neurology) can describe certain phenomena related to the experience of dying, but they cannot explain the meaning of death. Noting these facts, Brunner n[illegible] poses the question, "What is death?" and seeks to provide the dictinctively Christian answer insofar as it can be ascertained on the basis of revelation. He points out that for man, and man alone, the whole of life is a "being unto death." Only man lives his life in anticipation of death and knows in some measure what he loses in that experience. Yet, the more man is aware of his subjective nature as a person, his radical distinction from other living creatures, the more impenetrable is the mystery of his death.[13]

As Brunner observes, the lower animals repel death by instinct, but man revolts against it. This revolt is deeper than the natural instinct for self-preservation; it grows out of the depths of the human spirit. Moreover, it has led to the widespread idea of a survival of the soul after the dissolution of the body. This essentially dualistic notion has found expression in such diverse systems of religious thought as the Indian doctrine of the law of *karma,* the Egyptian expectation of a transcendent judgment, and the Platonic idea of the immortality of the soul. Each of these systems of thought asserts in its own way a belief in the fundamental distinction between the personal being of man and nature.

The Platonic doctrine of the immortality of the soul, especially, has had profound effect upon the spiritual thought of the West, within both Roman Catholicism and Protestantism. Only in recent theology has its origin in pre-Christian idealistic philosophy and its basic incompatibility with the biblical conception of personality been noticed. A more adequate understanding of the New Testament shows that this doctrine does not take seriously the reality of death. Platonic philosophy presents man as a composite being and the soul (man's essential part) as untouchable by death. Death is here seen as merely the liberation of the immortal soul from an evil, sensuous body; it is not believed to touch man as a person. In effect, this teaching ignores the matter of personal responsibility. Moral evil is not regarded as a contradiction of the divine will, and therefore sin; it is rather understood as nothing more serious than a certain lethargy of spirit. In contrast to this Platonic conception of man is the consistent biblical view of him as a unity before God. Anything that touches him as a person touches his whole being.[14]

In the light of the foregoing discussion, Brunner now poses the question as to the *Christian* conception of death. He finds only limited help regarding the mystery of death in the Old Testament. It is there regarded as an ordinance of the Creator and as bearing a positive relation to sin. In some sense, it is indicative of man's responsibility before God. As to man's survival of death, the Old Testament, with rare exceptions, knows only of a shadowy, subterranean existence in Sheol. In the New Testament, however, Brunner finds a much more radical relation between sin and death. Here the two are in fact seen as a unity. Moreover, sin is here seen to involve the whole of human existence in its rebellion against God, bringing that life in its totality under the divine judgment. Here, the whole of life is but a "being unto death." But in the final analysis, it is only in personal encounter with the crucified Christ that the meaning of death stands exposed, and thereby also (and at the same moment) the meaning of sin.[15]

Human death includes, but is not identical with, physical death. Brunner speaks of it as "the death of the person." This death is by divine decree because of sin. Even for the Christian, there is still a residue of rebellion and therewith the reality of human death. Yet this death is contrary to the primal will of God, which is reasserted in the reconciling work of Jesus Christ. Brunner finds the Apostle Paul to be especially helpful here in his words: "For the law of the Spirit of life in Christ Jesus made me free from the law of sin and death" (Rom. 8:1–2). For the believer, therefore, physical death is in effect "to depart and be with Christ" (Phil. 1:23). And this means that for faith, the mystery of death is unveiled "in part"—until faith gives way to sight and hope to eternal Presence.

To "depart and be with Christ"—this is the way Paul spoke of his own death. In this expression, he seems to imply that the death of an individual believer is followed immediately by life with Christ. Yet, he can also speak, indeed in the same brief letter, of a coming of the Lord, "who shall fashion anew the body of our humiliation, that it may be conformed to the body of his glory" (Phil. 3:20–21). This latter reference is generally understood to imply a universal event in consummation of the sovereignty of God. The problem has arisen, therefore, as to whether Paul intended to suggest an individual or a universal form of eschatology. And this has led in turn to various speculative ideas as to what ensues immediately upon the death of an individual person.

Some theologians have held that at death one enters upon a state of soul sleep, thus to await a general resurrection at the last day. With that event, soul and body, it is believed, will be raised together. Others have held that at death, the disembodied soul immediately receives conscious life, but must await union with the resurrection body until the last day. Brunner believes that both of these interpretations have failed to discern that Paul's two statements were but different modes of expressing the same thing. He holds that for faith the paramount concern at the temporal frontier is not a curiosity as to what happens at death, for its eye is already fixed in hope upon the promise of the resurrection. And in any event it is pointless, Brunner believes, to dwell upon the separation of the event of one's death and that of the general resurrection, for separation in point of time cannot mean separation from the perspective of eternity.[16]

HOPE AS PAROUSIA AND RESURRECTION

Brunner understands the resurrection in the larger context of the *parousia,* the coming of the Lord in glory. *Parousia,* in the literal sense of the Greek word, means presence, an advent, a coming, and this in turn is the central theme of the entire Bible. The whole content of promise and fulfillment revolves around such ideas as the coming of the Messiah, the coming of the day of the Lord, and the coming of the Kingdom of God. What the Old Testament sees as promise, the New Testament sees as fulfillment. Moreover, in the New Testament, the coming of God is set forth in reference to all three dimensions of time. Here it is asserted as of equal significance that he has come, that he is present, and that he will come. And here again is expressed that unity in which the ecclesia has its existence, for in each dimension of time the point of reference is Christ who is the object in faith and love and hope. In each case it is Presence, Emmanuel—"God-with-us," a pronouncement which at very best can be made only in symbolic language.[17]

Brunner takes note of the fact that there are only "hints" of the idea of a resurrection of the dead in the Old Testament and that these all belong to the exilic and postexilic literary deposit. Even the great preexilic prophets show no concern for the individual person beyond the frontier of death, nor do they seem to know that the Kingdom of God extends beyond the range of historical existence. On the other hand, the idea of a resurrection is already at least a familiar subject in the New Testament period. These facts have led Brunner to the conviction that the conception of a resurrection of the dead came into Judaism by way of Persian religious influence.

In comparison with his dominant theme of the coming of the Kingdom of God, even Jesus shows only modest concern with the subject of individual resurrection. In this regard, however, it is important to note that for him, the Kingdom of God is an intrusion from beyond history. Only with the preaching of the apostles does the idea of the resurrection become the epicenter of the gospel message. These were the men "to whom he showed himself alive after his passion by many proofs, appearing unto them by the space of forty days, and speaking the things concerning the kingdom of God" (Acts 1:3). The profound impression of this encounter with the risen Lord is suggested in Paul's reminder to the Corinthians: "I delivered unto you first of all that which also I received: that Christ died for our sins . . . and that he was buried; and that he hath been raised on the third day" (1 Cor. 15:3–4).[18]

Brunner speaks of the resurrection of Jesus as an "eschatological fact," an "utterly incomprehensible and transcendent" event. He sees it as "the beginning of the Parousia," an "inbreak of the eternal world of God into our temporal sphere." It is in this light that he understands the discrepancies which are apparent in the various reports of these things by the primitive witnesses themselves. In their spatio-temporal existence, there simply were no means adequate to describe what they had seen. As one of them put it: "we beheld his glory" (John 1:14). Of one thing they were very sure, namely, that with the appearance of the risen Lord, the new age had dawned.[19]

In his own understanding of this subject, Brunner begins with the New Testament witness to two realities: the fact of the resurrection of Jesus, and the unmistakable newness of life in the Holy Spirit which marked those who beheld and believed. Both of these facts are conceived to be of inestimable importance for the judgment that the new age had begun. Both are regarded as irrefutable evidence that the future and the eternal had in fact invaded the present. Henceforth, the life of individual believers and that of the ecclesia are in essence seen as life in the power of the Holy Spirit and are regarded as resurrection life. Yet, they are so meanwhile only in hiddenness, for that life is still manifest in this world through the medium of an old sin-laden existence. Brunner affirms nevertheless that already the "being unto death" is changed to a being unto life, even though this transformation is as yet only provisional in character. The full realization of the believer's true destiny must await his own resurrection, whereby he will be perfectly conformed to the image and the presence of God. And that experience must await the event of the final coming of the Lord in glory.

Every man must pass through physical death, but one of the most obvious manifestations of the new life in Christ, for Brunner, is its certainty of the resurrection. In this hope, death has indeed lost its sting. He holds, however, that the New Testament knows nothing of a resurrection of the flesh. It speaks only of a spiritual body in the resurrection, yet one of such character as to preserve and express the wholeness of personality and individuality. Brunner finds these ideas authenticated in Paul's Corinthian correspondence, according to which "flesh and blood cannot inherit the kingdom of God" (1 Cor. 15:50). And in reference to the death of the body, this apostle also observes that "it is sown a natural body; it is raised a spiritual body" (1 Cor. 15:44). The promise of a resurrection body, Brunner believes, is indicative of the fact that to all eternity the life of the redeemed will be marked by fellowship, worship, and love.[20] The body is instrumental to that end.

Thus, according to Brunner, we may assert only the fact of the resurrection. We know nothing of the how of it. There are, however, certain related subjects which are already implied in what has been said thus far. These are both personal and cosmic in range. Something must now be said regarding these matters.

OTHER MATTERS RELATED TO ETERNAL HOPE

The Last Judgment and the Question of Universal Redemption

Thus far, Brunner's theme has been the self-movement of God in love toward his creation. He has spoken often of the coming of the Kingdom of God, but always with the conscious reservation that it may appear within the context of history only in veiled form. Now, he is ready to speak of the advent of the Kingdom in the fullness of its glory, which means the end of history, the fulfillment of human history, and the bringing of all history to judgment.

Brunner finds that in all parts of the Bible the idea of judgment stands in close correlation to that of the coming of the holy God to a sinful world. In the Old Testament, it is almost always conceived of as something which occurs within history and in relation to particular historical circumstances. Moreover, it is generally corporate in character and application, only gradually becoming discriminatory in a personal and individualized sense. In the New Testament, the idea of judgment becomes much more radical in several respects. It is individual and personal in character, universal in scope, and eschatological in meaning. In the Old Testament, judgment is declared in strict accordance with things as they are. In the New Testament it is accompanied by the creation of a new state of affairs in the forgiveness of sin.[21]

In taking up the theology of judgment, Brunner is aware of a kind of ambiguity in the New Testament references to this subject. Jesus seemed to advocate a radical reversion of the standards of judgment. Whereas the Old Testament had made righteousness and unrighteousness the paramount point of distinction in matters of divine judgment, Jesus proclaimed that "the publicans and harlots" would precede the self-righteous Pharisees into the Kingdom of God, and that on the basis of belief alone. Paul pursued this idea to its logical conclusion in his doctrine of justification by grace through faith, yet without abandoning the place and meaning of works. He exhorted the Corinthians, for example, to be "stedfast, unmovable, always abounding in the work of the Lord, forasmuch as ye know that your labor is not in vain in the Lord" (1 Cor. 15:58). A similar attitude is also found in the writings of John, but with the additional thought that for one who believes in Christ the judgment has already taken place. He quotes Jesus as saying: "Verily, verily, I say unto you, he that heareth my word, and believeth him that sent me, hath eternal life, and cometh not into judgment but hath passed out of death into life" (John 5:24).

Brunner finds throughout the varied witness of the New Testament one consistent and fundamental idea—that judgment is the necessary corollary of the holiness of God. This belief, he holds, is founded upon divine revelation. Moreover, the Christ-event in a sinful world is understood as having already brought crisis and judgment to men within the framework of history. But final judgment, like the conquest of evil itself, must await the coming of Christ in glory, when all things will be brought to light and a final decisive separation will take place between good and evil.[22]

From this point onward, Brunner's precise thought becomes somewhat difficult to follow. He attempts to bring forward his emphasis upon human responsibility and the authenticity of personal decision-making; yet he seems to say that man can really do no more than endorse a prior decision which God has already made in his behalf. He affirms that God's self-revelation is a call to decision, but he goes on to declare that this does not mean a choosing between alternative possibilities. God has already claimed man for his own. Freedom before God, therefore, consists in the fact that man may assent to the prior divine decision which has been made regarding him. Brunner refers to man's own decision as "merely the echo, the subsequent completion" of the primal divine Word whereby he has already been claimed unconditionally. He pursues this argument further by reference to the apocalyptic passage in Matthew 25:31–46. The traditional interpretation of this passage portrays a last judgment in which two alternatives (salvation or damnation) are set forth in "static symmetry." Brunner believes that this was not the intention of Jesus. He understands these words of the Lord rather as living and dynamic and therefore "asymmetrical and anti-static" in character. They are taken to imply God on the move toward us, with a view to the determination of our movement in his direction.

Brunner sees the entire evangelical message of the New Testament as asymmetrical and alogical in character. On the one hand, he finds a message of judgment, which suggests "a twofold issue of world history." But on the other hand, he finds a proclamation of forgiveness and grace in universal atonement, which seems to suggest that the outcome of history is uniform. He holds that in their obsession with "the ideal of firm doctrine," theologians have generally failed to make allowance for this paradoxical aspect of the one message. As a result, they have arbitrarily chosen one or the other of two possibilities: the way of judgment with a final separation of good and evil, or the way of universal atonement. When pushed to their logical extremes, the first of these views leads ultimately to a doctrine of double predestination and the second to a doctrine of universalism.

Brunner holds that the way of faith is not that of simply choosing between these two biblical emphases. Both must be heard as the Word of God, and as a Word of challenge rather than of formulated doctrine. Faith lives by repeatedly passing through judgment to grace. This is another way of saying that the truth of God's Word is always formative, subjective, and personal. One is in the truth only in an awareness of both the sovereignty and the love of God. In recognition of the emphasis on divine judgment, one learns the meaning of the fear and reverence of God. In recognition of the emphasis on universal redemption, he learns the meaning of the love of God. And only so may one grasp and hold in perspective the duality of holiness and love in the one being of the God who comes to us.[23]

The Consummation of All Things

Brunner holds that the ultimate purpose of God in his divine self-movement is his own glorification. This is a theme, therefore, which is more suited to the act of worship than to theologizing, and more adequately expressed in doxology than in formal prose. It cannot for that reason be simply abandoned by the theologian, however, for all of the key strands of his multiform structure merge at this point.

In the New Testament, creation, redemption, and consummation are brought together as the expression of the mystery of the divine will. The classic statements of this truth are Ephesians 1:9–23, Colossians 1:13–23, and the Prologue to the Gospel of John. All of these find their ground and meaning in Jesus Christ in whom God has purposed "to sum up all things . . . the things in the heavens, and the things upon the earth . . . to the end that we should be unto the praise of his glory, we who had before hoped in Christ" (Eph. 1:10–12). Brunner holds that the Christian faith stands or falls on the proposition that Christ is the goal of the world, for in him, and through him, and into him was it created (cf. Col. 1:16–20). And finally, Brunner observes that it is as impossible for us to represent to ourselves the end of the world as it is to imagine creation out of nothing. It is directed toward the realization of the divine will in God's purpose in the creation.[24]

IX. Brunner's Theology in Retrospect

SOME GENERAL OBSERVATIONS

The foregoing chapters are an attempt to render the essence of Brunner's theology as fully and faithfully as possible within the necessary limitations of space. In view of the vast range of his thought and the extensive volume of his work, some omissions and inadequacies have been inevitable in this modest presentation of his system. The aim throughout this work, therefore, has been to keep as close as possible to what is fundamental to his thought. Perhaps the more obvious deficiencies in this review of his work are related to the doctrine of creation and the doctrine of man. No separate treatment is here given to Brunner's doctrine of creation, though the principal aspects of his thought in this regard are set forth in connection with other subjects which are dealt with in some depth. More specifically, his understanding of creation is indicated in what is said with reference to revelation, God, man, and Christ. Again, only limited attention has been given to the subject of man in his various moral relations. And almost nothing is shown here of Brunner's fine studies of man as the builder of culture and civilization, or of the meaning of his being as a thinking Christian in the modern world.

In retrospect, several general observations may be made concerning Brunner and his theology. In the first place, he endeavors to retain a healthy and balanced orientation toward each of the three dimensions of time. With reference to the past, he finds his roots embedded in the Bible, the central stream of Christian history, and the great confessions of the church. With reference to the present, he manifests a critical openness to the full range of modern scholarship and a sensitive rapport with modern man in his struggle for authentic existence. With reference to the future, he demonstrates faith in the continuing activity of God in the world and believing hope in the ultimate triumph of the divine purpose of history.

For Brunner, Christian theology is a product of constant and faithful encounter with a reality which must be apprehended anew in every age. God himself does not change, nor does the content of the gospel, but the situation in which man has his existence does change. The theologian, therefore, must be in living touch with both the changing and the unchanging and equally discerning of both. Brunner understands dogmatics as something which takes place primarily in and for the believing community. Yet, he insists upon the evangelical and missionary character of the faith. And this means that theology must play a servant role in the church and in the world. Moreover, it means for Brunner that a viable theology must be in living relation to all that God is doing in the world.

Again, for Brunner, there can be no valid theology which is not firmly based upon and limited by divine revelation. Theology begins and ends with the fact of the self-movement of God and the realization of the eternal purpose toward which he moves. That divine purpose includes a primal Word in which man has his origin, his existence, and his destiny. It has its possibility in the fact that God has created and sustained in man a "point of contact" whereby that Word may be received. It has its actuality in the fact that Christ has become the mediator of creation, of revelation, and of redemption. It has its fulfillment in that consummation toward which all things move under the lordship of Christ.

Brunner builds his whole system around certain dynamic concepts, such as personhood, personal correspondence, truth as encounter, divine orders of creation, and ecclesia as fellowship. He is convinced that neither the essence of faith, the content of love, nor the substance of hope is reducible to mere doctrines. They must be lived before there can be any valid formulation of their meaning. For him, it is unthinkable that theology should be undertaken in isolation, apart from the practice of faith. In consequence of this approach, Brunner has succeeded in presenting a theology which speaks equally to the head and to the heart. It is existential in the best sense of that term, not as arising from the side of man, but as representing at every point an encounter with the living God.

SOME LINGERING QUESTIONS

Thus far, no attempt has been made in this review to take issue with any of the ideas of Brunner. And before such an undertaking is entered upon, I should like to register profound and abiding gratitude for the thought of this superb Christian thinker. In many respects I can identify more closely with his theology than with that of any of the other great system builders of this century. This is not to say, however, that no questions have arisen in the process of analyzing his thought. Certain questions have indeed arisen, some of which have been pointed out previously by others. On the other hand, I believe that adverse judgments regarding aspects of Brunner's thought have sometimes been too hastily formed, without hearing him out to the end. It seems in order at this point, therefore, to call attention to some matters in his thought concerning which reservations persist and in some cases to react to criticisms which have been put forward regarding aspects of his theology.

Perhaps the first word to be said at this point should be directed at the very idea of a comprehensive *system* of theology. Brunner is by any reasonable standard of judgment one of the three or four great system builders of this century.[1] But just as his career was drawing to a close, the idea of a system (especially a one-man system) was being seriously questioned by a vocal segment of the younger theologians, particularly those of this country. For an age of analysis and specialization, the idea of an orderly system became more and more suspect, if not actually presumptuous. Not only did it appear audacious in scope, it also seemed to focus too much upon positions already secured. While the great systems were in process, for example, nothing seemed incongruous about the *Christian Century* decennial series of articles on the subject, "How My Mind Has Changed" in the past ten years.[2] In a later series of articles, the younger theologians felt more comfortable with the caption, "How I Am Making Up My Mind."[3] They preferred to represent themselves as men engaged in ardent quest. This new outlook is probably reflected in recent years in the diminishing emphasis upon systematic theology in the curricula of some theological schools, evidence for which one need only examine a variety of current catalogues.

In this regard, one can appreciate the misgivings which have been expressed on both counts. An awesome and ever-increasing scope of learning is demanded for the construction of a balanced system which can address itself to the deepening complexities of man in the modern world. And again, there is a diminishing level of confidence in some theological answers which once seemed valid for all time. On the other hand, the composite character of the Christian faith renders it liable to corruption unless all of its concerns are held in true perspective. There is a perpetual danger that in isolating and treating of certain aspects of the faith, one may do violence to other matters of equal importance. One is of the opinion, therefore, that in some form the system must continue to be a part of the theological scene.

Another point in question has to do with Brunner's understanding of nature and grace. He is surely right, I believe, in his insistence upon a measure of revelation in nature, in the human conscience, and in history. And he is also right in contending against Barth that there is still in sinful man a "point of contact" for the grace of redemption. But the question arises as to whether he goes far enough in these matters. The universal desire of the human spirit for the supernatural and the uneasy conscience because of sin are indications that all men have been confronted and disturbed in some measure by the Spirit of God. John Baillie's appraisal of Brunner's thought in this regard seems fair and discerning. He believes that Brunner distinguishes too sharply between form and content in reference to the image of God in man, between goodness and reasonableness in human activity, and between sustaining grace and saving grace in divine activity.[4] There must of course be no diminishing of the significance of the supreme and complete divine revelation in Christ, nor must there be any detraction from the meaning of his atoning death. But neither must there be any discounting of the fact of the continuous and universal and purposeful activity of God in the world.

Again, Brunner regards his work as a biblical theology,[5] rejecting whatever is deemed to be without clear support in the Scriptures. There are, however, two observations one would make with regard to his handling of the doctrine of the Scriptures as the record of the special divine revelation. The first has to do with the matter of inspiration. He rightly regards inspiration as only one aspect of the larger doctrine of revelation and feels that any attempt to indicate the how of it leads to an unwarranted speculative theory, such as that expressed in the plenary verbal view.[6] It would seem, however, that just as he was not deterred from dealing with the fact of creation and the fact of revelation (without attempting to state the how of either), he might have said more about the meaning of inspiration for the production and preservation of Scripture. It is difficult to see how this would have compromised his view that revelation is "truth as encounter" or that faith is "knowledge as encounter." After all, there must be some solid basis for insistence upon the authority of Scripture for valid theology.

Another question arises frequently in reference to Brunner's use of Scripture. There are times when he seems almost arbitrary in asserting what is biblical and what is not. He seems to assume the biblical character of certain ideas (for example, the *creatio ex nihilo*—creation out of nothing—and the *imago Dei)* on the basis of a very few references. Other matters considered of significance in traditional Christian doctrine are discredited if not outright rejected, in part, at least, upon the basis that they are not more widely supported in Scripture. Among the latter may be mentioned his disposition of the idea of the virgin birth of Jesus and his regard for the report of the open tomb on Easter morning. For Brunner, the final judgment concerning the authenticity of these matters is obviously rational in character, despite his usual aversion to this principle of grounding knowledge.

One of the finest and most widely acclaimed parts of Brunner's work is his doctrine of man. He seems to have expended far more labor on this division of his system than on any other, producing several volumes on different aspects of it. Probably his most significant contribution in this area is that which has been dealt with in this review under the caption "Man in Society." Two general questions may be raised here, however. In the first place, one wonders how precise Brunner intends to be in his use of the term *ethics.* He speaks of "the problem of ethics," as having been already raised "the moment that human consciousness exists," for at that point a decision is demanded as to right conduct. To live and act "with a human consciousness," he says, is to do so "ethically." The ethical problem of right conduct is declared to belong intrinsically to human existence. "Theoretically," he asserts, "we may evade the ethical question, practically we *cannot.*" And he adds that there are two kinds of ethics: "that which is actually lived and recognized in life," and that which is "theoretically formulated." [7] Yet, in a later chapter he contends that not all men have an ethic, that many groups of civilized men are rather characterized by "moral systems." Here, he confines the possession of an ethic to that "sphere of civilization" which has been "determined by Hellenism and Christianity." [8]

Perhaps Brunner means simply to suggest a distinction between ethics as theory and systems of morality as practice, for he does say that the moral "precedes every kind of ethic." Even so, his intention is not entirely clear at this point. One wonders if this is not another instance of distinguishing too sharply between form and content in the determination of what is representative of an ethic. It might be pointed out that even before a particular group is touched by the Hellenistic and Christian influences, there may be a vast deposit of proverbs which reflect a high level of contemplation as to the meaning of human existence and relations.

In the second place, one believes that Brunner has left himself open to criticism in his radical distinction between justice and love. He finds the basis of justice to be both realistic and rational and therefore comprehensible to everyone. But by the same token, it is also impersonal and belongs inherently to an impersonal system. In a world where there are systems, he believes that justice is as indispensable as love and is in no way inferior to it. Love, on the other hand, is superrational, incomprehensible, and intensely personal. The more narrow the scope of an institution number-wise, the greater is the possibility of love. In a marriage, for example, there is the possibility of love, whereas in a state there is only the possibility of justice. And in any instance, justice is the precondition of love, which begins where justice has reached its limits. Justice can be satisfied; love never can.[9]

Brunner is aware that in so stating the case between justice and love, he is not taking the "document of revelation" as his starting point.[10] He is rather using the term *justice* in the modern sense of the word. But as Paul Ramsey points out, in so doing, he seriously narrows the meaning of justice in the light of its biblical usage. Ramsey believes that in Old Testament thought, the nation of Israel, with all of its institutions, was under covenantal compulsion "to serve the cause of justice" in the fullest meaning of that term. This required that a distinction be made between the judgmental righteousness (the *tsedeq)* of God on the one hand and human justice (or *mishpat)* on the other, but to do so in such a way that the former become normative for the latter. Ramsey also points out that the righteous judgment (the *tsedeq)* of God also encompasses the idea of his saving activity. And on this basis, he asserts that the Bible knows little if any conflict between the idea of justice and that of love.[11]

Again, Brunner understands justice in terms of "things fixed" according to the "primal order" of creation. Man is seen as fitting into a definite structure which gives order to the whole of life. On this basis alone, he says, can one presume that something "belongs to him by right." Brunner does not hesitate to speak of man as being "fitted in" that structure and of his being "in a way . . . disposed of." In contrast to love, justice is here seen as having a statutory quality whereby it can serve as a norm for the judgment of impersonal relationships or laws or institutions. Justice is said to belong, therefore, to the ethics of institutions and systems, and here indeed to be "the supreme and ultimate standard." Love, on the other hand, is spoken of as belonging to the ethics of personhood.[12]

George F. Thomas points out that there is here an implied fallacy in the presumption that apart from love of neighbor, one may rightly determine what is just for him. Thomas holds that just as the will is corrupted by sin, so also is the reason distorted. Therefore, he contends, the corrupted reason cannot know the purpose of God for one's neighbor in the primal order of creation apart from the illumination of faith and the will to love. And these are based upon God's purpose of redemption made known through revelation. Love adds purpose to a system of justice and thus transforms it. One believes that this is a further valid argument against the radical distinction which Brunner sees between love and justice.[13]

As already indicated in the sixth chapter of this review, questions have been raised concerning Brunner's treatment of the church. He seems to have been aware that this segment of his thought did not gain the general acceptance to which he had become accustomed in his earlier writings and was puzzled and disappointed by that fact. Perhaps no part of his work has been more widely misunderstood than has this, and the reasons are not readily apparent, unless it be that there has been a failure to hear him through to the end. His theology of the ecclesia is surely continuous with his thought in general and in harmony with the fundamental propositions which undergird his system. Perhaps the difficulty here may stem from an unfortunate arrangement in his argument. It is only after he has presented a revolutionary challenge to the usual identity of the historical church and the ecclesia that he professed nevertheless to find that all along the former has been the "shell" and "vessel" of the latter.

A final question may be raised with regard to Brunner's discussion of the problem of the last judgment and the question of universal redemption. He is generally very lucid in his positions and in the arguments with which these are delineated, but his thought in this regard appears somewhat ambiguous.[14] He seems to be aware of the problem here, but as indicated in the previous chapter, he was seeking to do justice to a twofold emphasis which he sees in the Scriptures themselves. The result has been that while one of his strongest emphases throughout his theology is that of personal responsibility and accountability, he is sometimes (perhaps unjustly) thought to have finally advocated universal salvation. This, I believe, was not his intention; yet in the light of the cautious ambiguity of his language, the question lingers.

Notes

CHAPTER I

1. *The Japan Christian Quarterly*, July 1955, pp. 238–44, hereafter referred to as *JCC*.

2. Charles W. Kegley, ed., *The Theology of Emil Brunner* (New York: The Macmillan Company, 1962), p. 8. Cited hereafter as Kegley.

3. *JCC*, July 1966, p. 154.

4. The material in this section is based on Brunner's accounts as published in *JCC* and Kegley. Unless otherwise credited quotations are Brunner's own words.

5. Williston Walker, *A History of the Christian Church*, 2nd ed. (New York: Charles Scribner's Sons, 1959), p. 506, as well as *JCC*, July 1966, and Kegley.

6. Kegley, p. 8; *JCC*, July 1955, p. 242. The Scripture passage to which Brunner refers reads: "For I am not ashamed of the gospel of Christ: for it is the power of God unto salvation to every one that believeth" (KJV).

7. Kegley, pp. 355–84.

8. Emil Brunner, *Das Symbolishe in der Religiösen Erkenntnis* (Tübingen: J. C. B. Mohr, 1914).

9. Kegley, pp. 5–6.

10. Emil Brunner, *Erlebnis, Erkenntnis und Glaube* (Tübingen: J. C. B. Mohr, 1921).

11. Kegley, p. 9.

12. Cf. the article by Dale Moody in *The Review and Expositor*, 44, no. 3 (July 1947): 314–15.

13. Emil Brunner, *Die Mystik und das Wort* (Tübingen: J. C. B. Mohr, 1924).

14. See Kegley, p. 9. Cf. *JCC*, July 1955, pp. 241–42.

15. Kegley, p. 9.

16. Emil Brunner, *The Mediator,* trans. Olive Wyon (Philadelphia: The Westminster Press, 1947), p. 16.
17. Emil Brunner, *Religionsphilosophie evangelischer Theologie* (Munich: R. Oldenbourg, 1927). *The Philosophy of Religion from the Standpoint of Protestant Theology,* trans. A. J. D. Farrer and Bertram Lee Wolf (London: Ivor Nicholson and Watson, Ltd., 1937).
18. Brunner, *The Mediator,* p. 16.
19. *Der Mittler* (Tübingen: J. C. B. Mohr, 1927). See footnote 16 above.
20. Kegley, p. 9. Brunner's work on this subject preceded Karl Barth's in his *Die christliche Dogmatik im Entwurf* (Christian Dogmatics in Outline), which appeared in 1927.
21. Emil Brunner, *The Theology of Crisis* (New York: Charles Scribner's Sons, 1931). These were first given as the Swander Lectures in the Theological Seminary of the Reformed Church in the United States, at Lancaster, Pa. They were repeated in whole or in part in six other schools.
22. Emil Brunner, *Gott und Mensch* (Tübingen: J. C. B. Mohr, 1930). *God and Man,* trans. David Cairns (London: SCM Press, 1936).
23. Ibid., p. 9.
24. Emil Brunner, *The Word and the World* (London: SCM Press, 1931).
25. Ibid., pp. 5–7.
26. Kegley, p. 10.
27. Ibid., pp. 9–10.
28. Emil Brunner, *Das Gebot und die Ordnungen* (Tübingen: J. C. B. Mohr, 1932). *The Divine Imperative,* trans. Olive Wyon (Philadelphia: The Westminster Press, 1947).
29. See his *Von den Ordnungen Gottes* (On the Orders of God), *Vortrag im Berner Münster,* IV, 16S. (Bern: Gotthelf-Verlag, 1929); see also his "Die andere Aufgabe der Theologie," in *Zwischen,* 7, 1929, Heft 3.
30. Emil Brunner, *Natur und Gnade. Zum Gespräch mit Karl Barth* (Tübingen: J. C. B. Mohr, 1934).
31. Emil Brunner and Karl Barth, *Natural Theology,* trans. Peter Frankel (London: The Centenary Press, 1946). Cited hereafter as *Natural Theology.*
32. Emil Brunner, *Vom Werk des Heiligen Geistes* (Tübingen: J. C. B. Mohr, 1935).
33. Emil Brunner, *Unser Glaube* (Bern: Gotthelf-Verlag, 1935). *Our Faith,* trans. John W. Rilling (New York: Charles Scribner's Sons, 1936).
34. Kegley, p. 10.
35. Emil Brunner, *Der Mensch im Widerspruch* (Berlin: Furche-Verlag, 1937). *Man in Revolt,* trans. Olive Wyon (Philadelphia: The Westminster Press, 1947).

36. Kegley, pp. 11–12. This work preceded the anthropological works of Karl Barth and Reinhold Niebuhr.

37. Dean G. Peerman and Martin E. Marty, eds., *A Handbook of Christian Theologians* (Cleveland: The World Publishing Company, 1965), p. 421.

38. Emil Brunner, *Wahrheit als Begegnung* (Berlin: Furche-Verlag, 1938). The first English translation of this work (published by The Westminster Press, 1943) bore the title *The Divine-Human Encounter*, which failed to express the essential point of the book. In 1963, a revised and enlarged edition appeared in German and was reissued the following year in English as *Truth as Encounter*, trans. Amandus W. Loos and David Cairns, 2nd rev. ed. (Philadelphia: The Westminster Press, 1963).

39. Emil Brunner, *Offenbarung und Vernunft: Die Lehre von der christlichen Glaubenserkenntnis* (Zurich: Zwingli-Verlag, 1941). *Revelation and Reason: The Christian Doctrine of Faith and Knowledge*, trans. Olive Wyon (Philadelphia: The Westminster Press, 1946).

40. Emil Brunner, *Die christliche Lehre von Gott* (Zurich: Zwingli-Verlag, 1946). *The Christian Doctrine of God*, trans. Olive Wyon (Philadelphia: The Westminster Press, 1950). Cited hereafter as *Dogmatics* I.

41. Emil Brunner, *Die christliche Lehre von Schöpfung und Erlösung* (Zurich: Zwingli-Verlag, 1950). *The Christian Doctrine of Creation and Redemption*, trans. Olive Wyon (Philadelphia: The Westminster Press, 1952). Cited hereafter as *Dogmatics* II.

42. Emil Brunner, *Die christliche Lehre von der Kirche, vom Glauben, und von der Vollendung* (Zurich: Zwingli-Verlag, 1960). *The Christian Doctrine of the Church, Faith and Consummation*, trans. David Cairns with T. H. L. Parker (Philadelphia: The Westminster Press, 1962). Cited hereafter as *Dogmatics* III.

43. *Dogmatics* I, p. vi.

44. See the main divisions of the tables of contents in the three volumes of the *Dogmatics*.

45. Emil Brunner, *Das Wort Gottes und der moderne Mensch* (Zurich: Zwingli-Verlag, 1947). *The Word of God and Modern Man*, trans. David Cairns (Richmond, Virginia: John Knox Press, 1964).

46. Emil Brunner, *Christianity and Civilization*, 2 vols. (New York: Charles Scribner's Sons, 1948, 1949).

47. Emil Brunner, *Das Missverständnis der Kirche* (Zurich: Zwingli-Verlag, 1951). *The Misunderstanding of the Church*, trans. Harold Knight (Philadelphia: The Westminster Press, 1953).

48. Emil Brunner, *Das Ewige als Zukunft und Gegenwart* (Zurich: Zwingli-Verlag, 1953). *Eternal Hope*, trans. Harold Knight (London: Lutterworth Press; Philadelphia: The Westminster Press, 1954).

49. Kegley, p. 17.

50. Ibid., pp. 7–61.

51. Ibid., p. 4.
52. Brunner believed himself to have been the first to call attention to the "epoch-making character" of Barth's *Römerbrief (Epistle to the Romans)*. Cf. his statement in Kegley, p. 8.
53. Kegley, p. 38.

CHAPTER II

1. As used here, phenomenology is the description and classification of things (in nature, history, and psychology) as they appear to man.
2. Epistemology is the study of knowledge with regard to its origin, nature, and validity, and with respect to its possibilities and limitations.
3. Kegley, pp. 99–105.
4. Ibid., pp. 333–34. Cf. Brunner's works *The Theology of Crisis*, pp. 23–44; and *The Word and the World*, pp. 5–34.
5. Brunner, *Revelation and Reason*, pp. ix, 3. See also Brunner, *God and Man*, pp. 38–69.
6. Brunner, *Revelation and Reason*, pp. 20–21. Cf. Brunner, *Dogmatics* I, pp. 15–21. See also, Emil Brunner, *The Scandal of Christianity* (Richmond, Va.: John Knox Press, 1965), pp. 9–28.
7. Brunner, *Revelation and Reason*, pp. 22–25. Cf. *Dogmatics* I, pp. 22–23.
8. Brunner, *Revelation and Reason*, pp. 25–32.
9. Kegley, p. 12.
10. Brunner, *Truth as Encounter*, pp. 3–4.
11. Brunner, *Revelation and Reason*, pp. 3–7; 362–74.
12. Ibid., pp. 7–8.
13. Ibid., pp. 8–11.
14. The Enlightenment was a philosophical movement of the eighteenth century, with a strong emphasis upon the powers of human reason.
15. Brunner, *Revelation and Reason*, pp. 11–12.
16. Cartesian philosophy refers to the thought which is associated with the French philosopher, René Descartes.
17. Brunner, *Truth as Encounter*, pp. 7–9.
18. In his development of these opposing philosophies, Brunner presents the thought of Johann Gottlieb Fichte (1762–1814) as representative of idealism and that of Auguste Comte (1798–1857) as representative of realism.
19. Brunner, *Truth as Encounter*, pp. 86–88.
20. Ibid., pp. 89–102; also, *Revelation and Reason*, pp. 32–37.
21. Brunner, *Truth as Encounter*, pp. 130; 88–89; 101–102; 21.
22. Ibid., pp. 111–30. Cf. *Revelation and Reason*, pp. 36–37.
23. Brunner, *Truth as Encounter*, pp. 118–19. Cf. *Revelation and Reason*, pp. 37–40; also, *Dogmatics* I, pp. 35–42.

24. Brunner, *Truth as Encounter*, pp. 132–33.
25. Ibid., pp. 137–38; also, *Dogmatics* I, pp. 35–42.
26. Brunner, *Dogmatics* I, pp. 29–34; *Revelation and Reason*, pp. 164–84; and *Truth as Encounter*, pp. 137–40.
27. Brunner, *Truth as Encounter*, pp. 140–42. Cf. *Revelation and Reason*, pp. 42–44.
28. Brunner, *Dogmatics* I, pp. 303–20. Cf. *Truth as Encounter*, pp. 142–45.
29. Brunner, *Truth as Encounter*, pp. 145–52; also, *Revelation and Reason*, pp. 51–57.
30. Brunner, *Truth as Encounter*, pp. 153–60.
31. Ibid., pp. 161–73.
32. Ibid., pp. 174–76.
33. Ibid., pp. 176–77.
34. Ibid., pp. 178–81.
35. For a discussion of Luther's developing thought regarding faith and infant baptism, see Paul Althaus, *The Theology of Martin Luther*, trans. Robert C. Schultz (Philadelphia: Fortress Press, 1963), pp. 364–70.
36. Brunner, *Truth as Encounter*, pp. 181–89. Cf. *Dogmatics* III, pp. 53–84; also, *The Misunderstanding of the Church*, pp. 74–83.
37. Brunner, *Truth as Encounter*, pp. 189–99. Cf. *Dogmatics* III, pp. 58–72; also, *The Misunderstanding of the Church*, pp. 84–93.
38. Emil Brunner and Karl Barth, *Nature and Grace*. See chapter I, footnote 39.
39. Ibid., pp. 15–34. Cf. *Dogmatics* II, pp. 55–61; *Man in Revolt*, pp. 82–113; *Revelation and Reason*, pp. 218–36; and *The Word and the World*, p. 7.

CHAPTER III

1. Emil Brunner, *I Believe in the Living God*, trans. John Holden (Philadelphia: The Westminster Press, 1961). This was first published as *Ich glaube an den lebendigen Gott* (Zurich: Zwingli-Verlag, 1945).
2. Brunner, *God and Man*, pp. 38–46. Cf. *Dogmatics* I, pp. 151–56; *The Scandal of Christianity*, pp. 29–50.
3. Brunner, *God and Man*, pp. 44–54. Cf. *Dogmatics* I, pp. 151–56.
4. Brunner, *God and Man*, pp. 54–60. Cf. *Dogmatics* I, pp. 117–50; also, *Our Faith*, pp. 11–16.
5. Brunner, *God and Man*, pp. 62–64. Cf. *Dogmatics* III, p. 355.
6. Brunner, *God and Man*, pp. 64–66. Cf. *Dogmatics* I, pp. 141–42.
7. Brunner, *God and Man*, pp. 66–69. Cf. *Truth as Encounter*, pp. 18–30; 91–102.
8. Brunner, *Dogmatics* I, pp. 117–20. Cf. *Revelation and Reason*, pp. 88–90.

9. Brunner, *Dogmatics* I, pp. 120–28. Cf. *Revelation and Reason*, pp. 88–90.
10. Brunner, *Dogmatics* I, pp. 137–50. Cf. *The Scandal of Christianity*, pp. 9–28.
11. Brunner, *Dogmatics* I, pp. 157–67.
12. Ibid., pp. 183–91.
13. See Brunner, *The Scandal of Christianity*, p. 33. Cf. *Dogmatics* I, p. 199.
14. Brunner, *Dogmatics* I, pp. 205–9.
15. Brunner, *The Scandal of Christianity*, pp. 48–50. Cf. *Dogmatics* I, pp. 209–17.
16. Brunner is referring here to certain Platonic ideas which were incorporated into the Christian understanding of the faith in the second and third centuries and to certain Neo-Platonic ideas which were incorporated in the early fifth century.
17. *Dogmatics* I, pp. 248–55.
18. Pantheism is the belief that God pervades all things, and that ultimately God and nature are identical.
19. *Dogmatics* I, pp. 256–65.
20. Ibid., pp. 266–71.
21. Ibid., pp. 271–81.
22. Ibid., pp. 281–85.
23. Ibid., pp. 285–87.
24. Ibid., p. 303.
25. Ibid., pp. 304–13.
26. Ibid., pp. 313–39.

CHAPTER IV

1. Kegley, p. 331.
2. Brunner, *Man in Revolt*, pp. 60–83.
3. Ibid., pp. 449–501. Cf. *The Word of God and Modern Man*, pp. 12–15. Brunner points out that specific references to the *imago Dei* occur only three times in the Old Testament (in Gen. 1:26 ff.; 5:1; and 9:6), two times in the Apocrypha (in The Wisdom of Solomon 2:23; and Ecclesiasticus 17:3), and two times in the New Testament (in 1 Cor. 11:7; and James 3:9). He believes that certain other New Testament passages suggest a transformation of the meaning of the term *imago* from a rigid morphological interpretation to that of a "being-in-the-Word-of-God through faith." Brunner refers to this radically new interpretation of the term as "the basic idea of my whole work." The passages in question include Rom. 8:20; 2 Cor. 3:18; Eph. 4:24; and Col. 3:10.
4. Brunner, *Dogmatics* II, pp. 57–59.
5. Brunner, *Truth as Encounter*, p. 148.

6. Brunner, *Man in Revolt,* pp. 84–105.
7. In so naming his major work on anthropology, Brunner described the situation of man before God.
8. Brunner, *Dogmatics* II, pp. 89–90.
9. Ibid., p. 90. Brunner points out that Augustine's doctrine of sin and the fall focuses upon the deed of Adam and two related presuppositions, namely: that Adam is the physical father of the race; and, that sin is inherited.
10. Brunner, *Man in Revolt,* p. 132.
11. Ibid., pp. 137–42.
12. Ibid., pp. 145–52; see also, *Dogmatics* II, pp. 89–95.
13. Brunner, *Man in Revolt,* pp. 155–63.
14. Ibid., pp. 163–69.
15. Ibid., pp. 170–204; see also, *Dogmatics* II, pp. 118–32.
16. Brunner, *The Divine Imperative,* p. 9.
17. Ibid., pp. 10–13.
18. Ibid., pp. 17–19.
19. Ibid., pp. 21–28.
20. Ibid., pp. 29–33.
21. Deism is the doctrine that the creator of the universe is a personal God, but that he has removed himself from it and no longer exerts any control or influence over it.
22. Eudaemonism is that system of ethics which interprets moral obligation in terms of happiness or personal well-being.
23. Immanence is the doctrine that God is separable from yet indwells the world and man.
24. Brunner, *The Divine Imperative,* pp. 35–43.
25. Brunner points out the impressive ethical thought of Kant in particular as evidence in support of his argument that the problem of the good cannot be solved within the context of the philosophical ethic of reason.
26. Brunner, *The Divine Imperative,* pp. 50–52; see also, *God and Man,* pp. 76–80.
27. Brunner, *The Divine Imperative,* pp. 53–55.
28. Ibid., pp. 55–56.
29. Ibid., pp. 56–60.
30. Ibid., pp. 61–67.
31. Ibid., pp. 67, 82–89.
32. Ibid., pp. 68–81; see also, *God and Man,* pp. 85–90.
33. Brunner, *God and Man,* pp. 90–91.
34. Brunner, *The Divine Imperative,* pp. 111–13.
35. Ibid., pp. 114–51.
36. Ibid., pp. 151–78.
37. Ibid., pp. 179–218.
38. Ibid., pp. 218–33. Brunner's radical distinction between justice and love is set out in full in his somewhat controversial work, *Justice*

and the Social Order, trans. Mary Huttinger (New York: Harper & Bros. 1945).

39. Brunner, *The Divine Imperative*, pp. 234–62.
40. Ibid., pp. 269–74.
41. Ibid., pp. 278–79.

CHAPTER V

1. Brunner, *The Mediator*, pp. 13–17.
2. Ibid., pp. 122–52.
3. Ibid., pp. 21–41. Brunner believes that the rejection of the idea of the need for a mediator is characteristic of the theologies of such men as Schleiermacher, Ritschl, Harnack, and the adherents of the history of religions school. See ibid., pp. 42–71.
4. Brunner, *Dogmatics* II, pp. 171–273. Cf. *Dogmatics* I, p. 210.
5. *The Mediator*, pp. 399–402.
6. Ibid., pp. 402–12.
7. Ibid., pp. 416–31. Cf. *Dogmatics* II, pp. 275–81.
8. Brunner, *The Mediator*, pp. 435–40. Cf. *The Scandal of Christianity*, pp. 75–87; also, *Dogmatics* II, pp. 286–90.
9. Brunner, *The Mediator*, pp. 441–46. Cf. *Dogmatics* II, pp. 281–82.
10. Brunner, *The Mediator*, pp. 446–54. Cf. *Dogmatics* II, pp. 291–97.
11. Brunner, *The Mediator*, p. 455. Cf. *Dogmatics* II, pp. 283–85.
12. Brunner, *The Mediator*, pp. 456–74.
13. Ibid., pp. 490–510.
14. Ibid., pp. 515–28.
15. Ibid., pp. 561–63. For a further discussion of the dominical work of Christ, see *Dogmatics* II, pp. 298–305.
16. Brunner, *The Mediator*, pp. 584–90. After presenting the revealing, the reconciling, and the dominical work of Christ in distinction one from the other for purposes of clarity, Brunner finally also indicates their interrelatedness. He sees them as different aspects of the one reality. Cf. *Dogmatics* II, pp. 305–7.
17. Brunner, *The Mediator*, pp. 201–14. Cf. *Dogmatics* II, p. 322.
18. Brunner, *The Mediator*, pp. 220–31. Cf. *Dogmatics* II, pp. 327–29.
19. *The Mediator*, pp. 232–48.
20. Ibid., pp. 265–74. Cf. *Dogmatics* II, pp. 330–34. See also, *The Word of God and Modern Man*, pp. 47–51.
21. Brunner, *The Mediator*, pp. 275–78. Cf. *The Scandal of Christianity*, pp. 32–33. See also, *Dogmatics* II, pp. 334–36.
22. Brunner, *The Mediator*, p. 279.
23. Ibid., pp. 280–84. Cf. *Dogmatics* II, p. 340.
24. Brunner, *The Mediator*, pp. 285–91.
25. Ibid., pp. 291–302.

26. Ibid., pp. 303–15.
27. Ibid., p. 316.
28. Ibid., pp. 318–20. See also, *Dogmatics* II, pp. 343–50.
29. Brunner, *The Mediator*, pp. 320–27. Cf. *Dogmatics* II, pp. 350–56.
30. Brunner, *The Mediator*, pp. 328–37. Cf. *Dogmatics* II, pp. 357–63.
31. Brunner, *The Mediator*, pp. 338–45. Cf. *Dogmatics* II, pp. 239–363. By "the communication of properties" is meant the transference of what belongs essentially to one nature in Christ to the other nature in him—as for example, the transference to his human nature that which belongs essentially to his divine nature.
32. Brunner, *The Mediator*, pp. 345–76.

CHAPTER VI

1. Emil Brunner, *Die Kirchen, die Gruppenbewegung und die Kirche Jesu Christi* (Berlin: Furche-Verlag, 1936); *The Church and the Oxford Group*, trans. David Cairns (London: Hodder and Stoughton, 1937).
2. Brunner, *The Divine Imperative*, pp. 523–38.
3. Brunner, *The Misunderstanding of the Church*, p. 6.
4. Ibid., pp. 6, 10, 17.
5. Brunner, *Dogmatics* III, pp. 58–60.
6. Ibid., pp. 60–69.
7. Ibid., pp. 69–70.
8. Ibid., pp. 70–72.
9. Ibid., pp. 73–84.
10. Brunner, *The Misunderstanding of the Church*, pp. 116–18; cf. also, pp. 105–6.
11. Brunner, *Dogmatics* III, pp. 85–92.
12. Brunner, *The Misunderstanding of the Church*, pp. 10–13; and, *Dogmatics* III, pp. 3–18, 21–22. Brunner holds that dogmatics generally, as well as church leaders, lag far behind the research of the New Testament scholars in coming to an adequate understanding of the meaning of *ecclēsia* in primitive Christianity.
13. Ibid., pp. 22–27. Cf. also, *The Divine Imperative*, pp. 524–26.
14. Brunner, *Dogmatics* III, pp. 27–29. Luther was somewhat aware of the problem which is involved here and always manifested an aversion for the word *church*, but he did not distinguish clearly between ecclesia and church in the institutional sense.
15. Brunner, *The Misunderstanding of the Church*, p. 17.
16. Brunner, *Dogmatics* III, pp. 29–31. Brunner speaks of its visibility as one of the essential marks of the church. As such, it is a social reality. Yet, he speaks of it in another sense as being apprehended only in faith.

17. Ibid., pp. 31–36.
18. Ibid., pp. 37–40, 47.
19. Ibid., pp. 40–47. Cf. *God and Man,* pp. 107–12.
20. Brunner, *Dogmatics* III, pp. 47–52.
21. Also (and perhaps more accurately) known as the Niceno-Constantinopolitan Creed. This creed superseded the actual creed which was approved at Nicea.
22. Brunner, *Dogmatics* III, pp. 117–21.
23. Ibid., pp. 121–24.
24. Ibid., pp. 124–26.
25. Ibid., pp. 126–30.

CHAPTER VII

1. Brunner, *Dogmatics* III, pp. 134–39. Cf. *The Word and the World,* pp. 106–27.
2. See above chapter I, footnote 8.
3. Kegley, pp. 5–6.
4. See above chapter I, footnote 10.
5. Emil Brunner, *Faith, Hope and Love* (Philadelphia: The Westminster Press, 1956). These lectures were presented in the spring of 1955 as the Earl Lectures at the Pacific School of Religion at Berkeley, California.
6. Emil Brunner, *Der Römerbrief* (Kassel: J. G. Onken Verlag, 1938). *The Letter to the Romans,* trans. H. A. Kennedy (London: Lutterworth Press, 1959).
7. Brunner, *Dogmatics* III, pp. 132–335.
8. Ibid., p. 140. Brunner's full interpretation of Paul's understanding of faith is set forth in his discussion of the first eight chapters of Romans. See Brunner's *Letter to the Romans,* pp. 13–81.
9. Brunner, *Dogmatics* III, pp. 141–47.
10. Ibid., pp. 147–51.
11. Ibid., pp. 152–73.
12. See especially, Rom. 3:21–31.
13. Brunner finds the clearest instance of this in Gal. 3:23–25.
14. Brunner, *Dogmatics* III, pp. 173–75.
15. Ibid., pp. 176–78. Cf. *Truth as Encounter,* pp. 69, 119, and 139.
16. Brunner, *Dogmatics* III, pp. 178–90.
17. Ibid., p. 191.
18. Cf. Brunner's *Letter to the Romans,* pp. 28–32. One cannot avoid the feeling that Brunner prepared his entire treatment of faith with the Book of Romans lying open before him.
19. Brunner, *Dogmatics* III, pp. 191–211.
20. Ibid., pp. 269–75. Cf. *Our Faith,* pp. 103–6.
21. Brunner, *Our Faith,* pp. 99–103. Cf. *Dogmatics* III, p. 276.

22. Brunner, *Dogmatics* III, pp. 159–279.
23. Ibid., pp. 279–89.
24. Ibid., pp. 290–96.
25. Ibid., pp. 296–300.
26. Ibid., pp. 300–305.
27. Ibid., pp. 251–61.
28. Ibid., pp. 262–68.
29. Ibid., pp. 324–35.

CHAPTER VIII

1. Brunner, *Dogmatics* III, pp. 339–46. Cf. *Eternal Hope*, pp. 27–30.
2. See above, chapter VII, footnote 5.
3. Brunner, *Eternal Hope*, p. 7.
4. Brunner, *Dogmatics* III, pp. 339–40.
5. Brunner, *Eternal Hope*, p. 30.
6. Ibid., pp. 31–41.
7. Ibid., pp. 42–47.
8. Ibid., pp. 47–57.
9. Brunner, *Dogmatics* III, pp. 351–61.
10. Ibid., pp. 362–64.
11. Ibid., pp. 364–66.
12. Ibid., pp. 367–74.
13. Brunner, *Eternal Hope*, pp. 96–98; also *Dogmatics* III, pp. 381–83.
14. Brunner, *Dogmatics* III, pp. 383–84.
15. Ibid., pp. 385–87.
16. Ibid., pp. 387–93. Cf. *Eternal Hope*, pp. 108–13.
17. Brunner, *Eternal Hope*, pp. 136–41; also, *Dogmatics* III, pp. 394–98. On the theme of the Kingdom of God, see also *The Theology of Crisis*, pp. 108–13.
18. Brunner, *Eternal Hope*, p. 142; also *Dogmatics* III, p. 408. For Brunner's treatment of the offense of the idea of the resurrection, see *The Scandal of Christianity*, pp. 94–115.
19. Brunner, *Dogmatics* III, pp. 409–10. Cf. *Eternal Hope*, p. 144. See also Brunner's *I Believe in the Living God*, trans. John Holden (Philadelphia: The Westminster Press, 1961), pp. 151–60.
20. Brunner, *Eternal Hope*, pp. 144–54. Cf. *Dogmatics* III, pp. 411–14.
21. Brunner, *Eternal Hope*, pp. 155–71. Cf. *Dogmatics* III, p. 418. See also *Our Faith*, pp. 146–150.
22. Brunner, *Eternal Hope*, pp. 171–77.
23. Ibid., pp. 177–84. Cf. *Dogmatics* III, pp. 415–24.
24. Brunner, *Dogmatics* III, pp. 425–44.

CHAPTER IX

1. Cf. Daniel Day Williams, *What Present Day Theologians* Are *Thinking*, rev. ed. (New York: Harper & Brothers, Publishers, 1959), pp. 48–49.

2. These articles appeared in *The Christian Century* in coverage of three periods of ten years each, including the years 1928–1938, 1938–1948, and 1948–1958.

3. See Dean Peerman, ed., *Frontline Theology* (Richmond, Va.: John Knox Press, 1967).

4. See John Baillie, *Our Knowledge of God* (New York: Charles Scribner's Sons, 1959), pp. 28–34.

5. See Brunner, *Dogmatics* III, p. ix.

6. Brunner, *Revelation and Reason*, p. 9.

7. Brunner, *The Divine Imperative*, pp. 18–20.

8. Ibid., p. 34.

9. Brunner, *Justice and the Social Order*, pp. 125–30.

10. Ibid., p. 110.

11. Paul Ramsey, *Basic Christian Ethics* (New York: Charles Scribner's Sons, 1952), pp. 2–5; cf. also p. 13.

12. Brunner, *Justice and the Social Order*, pp. 19–20.

13. George F. Thomas, *Christian Ethics and Moral Philosophy* (New York: Charles Scribner's Sons, 1955), pp. 251–53. Cf. also E. Clinton Gardner, *Biblical Faith and Social Ethics* (New York: Harper & Bros., 1960), pp. 259–63.

14. This subject is also one which remains in ambiguity in Karl Barth's *Dogmatics*.

Selected Bibliography

I. WORKS BY EMIL BRUNNER

An exhaustive bibliography of Brunner's published works from 1914 to 1962 was compiled by his wife and appears in Charles W. Kegley (ed.), *The Theology of Emil Brunner* (New York: The Macmillan Company, 1962), pp. 355–82. In the same source is to be found a further bibliography prepared by Mrs. Brunner, listing her husband's principal works which have appeared in English.

A. Books

Christianity and Civilization. 2 vols. New York: Charles Scribner's Sons, 1948 and 1949.

The Church and the Oxford Group. Translated by David Cairns. London: Hodder and Stoughton, 1937.

The Divine Imperative. Translated by Olive Wyon. Philadelphia: The Westminster Press, 1947.

Dogmatics, Vol. I. *The Christian Doctrine of God*. Translated by Olive Wyon. Philadelphia: The Westminster Press, 1950.

Dogmatics, Vol. II. *The Christian Doctrine of Creation and Redemption*. Translated by Olive Wyon. Philadelphia: The Westminster Press, 1952.

Dogmatics, Vol. III. *The Christian Doctrine of the Church, Faith, and the Consummation*. Translated by David Cairns in collaboration with T. H. L. Parker. Philadelphia: The Westminster Press, 1962.

Eternal Hope. Translated by Harold Knight. Philadelphia: The Westminster Press, 1954.

Faith, Hope and Love. Philadelphia: The Westminster Press, 1956.

God and Man. Translated by David Cairns. London: SCM Press, 1936.

The Great Invitation. Translated by Harold Knight. London: Lutterworth Press, 1955.

I Believe in the Living God. Translated and edited by John Holden. Philadelphia: The Westminster Press, 1961.

Justice and the Social Order. Translated by Mary Hottinger. New York: Harper & Brothers, 1945.

The Letter to the Romans. Translated by H. A. Kennedy. London: Lutterworth Press, 1959.

Man in Revolt. Translated by Olive Wyon. Philadelphia: The Westminster Press, 1947.

The Mediator. Translated by Olive Wyon. Philadelphia: The Westminster Press, 1947.

The Misunderstanding of the Church. Translated by Harold Knight. Philadelphia: The Westminster Press, 1953.

"Nature and Grace." In: Emil Brunner and Karl Barth, *Natural Theology*. Translated by Peter Frankel. London: The Centenary Press, 1946.

Our Faith. Translated by John Rilling. New York: Charles Scribner's Sons, 1936.

The Philosophy of Religion. Translated by A. J. D. Farrer and Bertram Lee Woolf. London: Ivor Nicholson and Watson Limited, 1937.

Revelation and Reason. Translated by Olive Wyon. Philadelphia: The Westminster Press, 1946.

The Scandal of Christianity. Richmond, Virginia: John Knox Press, 1965.

The Theology of Crisis. New York: Charles Scribner's Sons, 1931.

Truth as Encounter. Translated by Amandus W. Loos, and David Cairns in consultation with T. H. L. Parker. Philadelphia: The Westminster Press, 1964.

Vom Werk des Heiligen Geistes. Zurich: Zwingli-Verlag, 1935.

The Word and the World. London: SCM Press, 1931.

The Word of God and Modern Man. Translated by David Cairns. Richmond, Virginia: John Knox Press, 1964.

B. Other Writings

"The Christian Sense of Time." In *The Wind and the Rain*. Translated by Joseph E. Cunneen. London: Publisher not given, 1951. Also printed as "Christian Understanding of Time." In *Scottish Journal of Theology* 4, no. 1 (1951) : 1–12.

"Church between East and West." In *Congregational Quarterly* 27 (July 1949) : 204–17.

The Church in the New Social Order. London: SCM Press, 1952.

Communism, Capitalism and Christianity. Translated by Norman P. Goldhawk. London: Lutterworth Press, 1949.

"Ecclesia and Evangelism." In *Japan Christian Quarterly* 21 (April 1955) : 154–9.

"Fresh Appraisal: the Cleveland Report on Red China." In *Christianity Today* 4 (April 25, 1960) : 3–6.

"New Barth." In *Scottish Journal of Theology* 4, no. 2 (1951): 123–35.
"Spiritual Autobiography." In *Japan Christian Quarterly* 21 (July 1955): 238–44.

II. WORKS ABOUT EMIL BRUNNER

A. Books

Allen, Edgar Leonard. *Creation and Grace: A Guide to the Thought of Emil Brunner*. New York: Philosophical Library, 1951.
Arnold, John James. *A Study of the Christologies of H. Emil Brunner and Gerrit C. Berkouwer*. Hartford, Connecticut: Unpublished Thesis, Hartford Seminary Foundation, 1967.
Heideman, Eugene Paul. *The Relation of Revelation and Reason in E. Brunner and H. Bavinck*. Assen, Netherlands: Van Gorcum & Comp. N.V., 1959.
Jewett, Paul K. *Emil Brunner: An Introduction to the Man and His Thought*. Chicago: Inter-Varsity Press, 1961.
———. *Emil Brunner's Concept of Revelation*. London: James Clarke & Co., Ltd., 1954.
Kegley, Charles W., ed. *The Theology of Emil Brunner*. New York: The Macmillan Company, 1962.
Nordquist, Roger Frank. *Emil Brunner on the Province of Reason*. New Haven: Unpublished Thesis, Yale University, 1966.
Rolston, Holmes. *A Conservative Looks to Barth and Brunner: An Interpretation of Barthian Theology*. Nashville, Tennessee: Cokesbury Press, 1933.
Schrotenboer, P. G. *A New Apologetics: An Analysis and Appraisal of the Eristic Theology of Emil Brunner*. Kampen, Netherlands: J. H. Kok, 1955.
Smith, Joseph J. *Emil Brunner's Theology of Revelation*. Manila: Loyola House of Studies, Atenco Manila University, 1967.
Van Til, Cornelius. *The New Modernism: An Appraisal of the Theology of Barth and Brunner*. Philadelphia: The Presbyterian and Reformed Publishing Company, 1946.

B. Other Writings

Boyd, M. "Point of Contact." In *Anglican Theological Review* 39 (January 1957): 70–81.
Cairns, D. "Theologians of Our Time: The Theology of Emil Brunner." In *Expository Times* 76 (November 1964): 55–8.
Cauthen, K. "Biblical Truths and Rational Knowledge." *Review and Expositor* 53 (October 1956): 467–76.
De Wolf, L. H. "Theological Rejection of Natural Theology: An Eval-

uation." *Journal of Religious Thought* 15 (Spring-Summer 1958): 91–106.

Douglass, Herbert Edgar. *Encounter with Brunner:* An Analysis of Emil Brunner's Proposed Transcendence of the Subjectivism-Objectivism Dichotomy in Its Relation to Christian Proclamation. Berkeley, California: Unpublished Thesis, Pacific School of Religion, 1964.

Furuya, Y. C. "Apologetic or Kerygmatic Theology." *Theology Today* 16 (January 1960): 471–80.

Hazelton, Roger. "Divine-Human Encounter." *Journal of Religious Thought* 14 (Spring-Summer 1957): 129–39.

Hendry, G. S. "Appraisal of Brunner's Theology." *Theology Today* 19 (January 1963): 523–31.

Horton, W. M. "Divine Imperative." *Congregational Quarterly* 35 (January 1957): 21–32.

Hughes, Phillip Edgecombe. "Myth in Modern Theology." *Christianity Today* 3 (March 30, 1957): 7–9.

Jewett, Paul K. "Emil Brunner and the Bible." *Christianity Today* 1 (January 21, 1957): 7–9.

McIntyre, J. "The Mediator." *Reformed Theological Review* 16 (1957): 11–20; 44–53.

Moody, Dale. "An Introduction to Emil Brunner." *The Review and Expositor* 44 (July 1947).

Nelson, J. R. "Emil Brunner: Teacher Unsurpassed." *Theology Today* 19 (January 1963): 532–5.

———. "Emil Brunner—The Final Encounter." *The Christian Century* April 20, 1966.

Reymond, Robert L. *Brunner's Dialectical Encounter*. Philadelphia: Presbyterian and Reformed Publishing Co., 1967.

Williams, S. W. "Social Thought of Emil Brunner." In *Journal of Religious Thought* 10 (1952–3): 34–43.